The Abingdon Women's Preaching Annual

Series 3
Year C

Compiled and Edited by

Beverly A. Zink-Sawyer

Abingdon Press
Nashville

THE ABINGDON WOMEN'S PREACHING ANNUAL

Copyright © 2003 by Abingdon Press

This book is printed on recycled, acid-free, elemental-chlorine–free paper.

ISBN 0-687-09574-3
ISSN 1086-8240

03 04 05 06 07 08 09 10 11 12 — 10 9 8 7 6 5 4 3 2 1

MANUFACTURED IN THE UNITED STATES OF AMERICA

For Steve

With gratitude for the grace and good humor

with which you endure being "the preacher's wife"

Contents

Introduction

September 15, 2003, will mark the 150th anniversary of the ordination of the first clergywoman. Antoinette Brown was ordained by a congregation affiliated with the Congregational Church in South Butler, New York. A young woman of twenty-eight, she had been called to serve the South Butler church after obtaining both her undergraduate and theological educations at Oberlin College in Ohio, the first college in the United States to admit women and among the first to admit African Americans. Despite Oberlin's open admissions policy, Brown had to fight for acceptance into the theology program. Many Oberlin students, faculty members, and, interestingly, faculty wives believed theology to be an inappropriate subject for female students. Undaunted, Brown completed work on a graduate degree in theology in 1850, even though her name would not appear in the official record of the theological class of 1850 until 1908 when she was invited back to Oberlin to be awarded the doctor of divinity degree.

Antoinette Brown's ordination occurred on a Sunday afternoon in the middle of a torrential rainstorm. Even the miserable weather, however, could not dampen the spirits of those who had gathered to witness such a monumental break with the customs of eighteen hundred years of Christian history. In addition to the members of the small, rural church that had called Brown to be their pastor, the gathering included local clergy and other influential leaders from New York and beyond, notably Gerrit Smith, the well-known abolitionist and philanthropist, and Dr. Harriot Hunt, one of the first women physicians in America. In a book of her memoirs, Dr. Hunt recalled the momentous occasion, one at which "even an equinoctial tempest could not detain me from being present." "There was something grand and elevating," Dr. Hunt remarked, "in the idea of a female presiding over a congregation, and breaking to them the bread of life—it was a new position for woman, and gave promise of her exaltation to that moral and intellectual rank, which she was designed to fill."[1]

Most historians of Christianity believe Antoinette Brown was the first woman ordained in terms of our modern understanding of ordination to the ministry of word and sacrament. Recent scholarship in the fields of church history and women's studies reveals glimpses of women's leadership in the church throughout its twenty centuries. Some women, especially in the very early years of the church, appear to have been set apart or recognized in some way for particular roles as church leaders, roles that may have been comparable to those of their male counterparts. In more recent centuries, women have led the church in many capacities, both official and unofficial. It was not until the mid–nineteenth century, however, that a few brave congregations and denominations followed the leading of the Spirit rather than the conventions of the times and ordained women to all the rights, privileges, and responsibilities of the clergy.

The anniversary of Antoinette Brown's ordination provides a unique opportunity to reflect on the remarkable work of women leaders in the church in centuries past. With the emergence of a discipline of women's studies over the past few decades, we now know more than ever before about the contributions of women to the life and work of the Christian church. That's the good news. The bad news is that there are still numerous and significant gaps in our knowledge. We know from anecdotal and historical evidence that there were countless women teaching, preaching, and serving the church in many different capacities throughout Christian history. We often *don't* know their names, however, or how they were regarded by church members and denominational hierarchies. We also have precious little of their written work. But bit by bit, sermon note by sermon note, journal entry by journal entry, historians are piecing together a portrait of women's service to the church and their witness to the gospel through the twenty centuries of Christian history.

Not long ago I taught a preaching workshop for commissioned lay pastors from my denomination. In the course of the workshop, I gave the participants a list of resources helpful to preachers. That list, of course, included the *Abingdon Women's Preaching Annual,* and I told them of my work with the current series. One of the participants raised his hand and asked, "Why a *women's* preaching annual?" I admit that the question, although a good one, caught me off guard. I have always taken for granted the value of work by women, especially in a field like preaching where women's voices have been absent for too long. And that is where I found the answer to that gentleman's question: in the importance of rectifying an ecclesiastical past deprived of women's voices and ensuring a future in which women are considered full and equal proclaimers of the gospel.

With this second volume of the third series of the *Abingdon Women's Preaching Annual,* we recognize and celebrate the gifts of women preachers in the church today. But works such as this do even more: They preserve women's voices so that they continue to echo through future generations of the church, inspiring and encouraging those who follow us on the road of Christian discipleship. I believe I speak for all the women represented in this volume when I express gratitude for the faith and witness of brave women like Antoinette Brown and the congregations and church leaders who supported them. At the same time, we all are mindful of those traditions and cultures that continue, even in the twenty-first century, to suppress or even vilify the gifts of women. Let us pray for the day when we all shall be one in Christ Jesus.

Beverly A. Zink-Sawyer
Ash Wednesday, 2002
Richmond, Virginia

---

1. Harriot K. Hunt, M.D., *Glances and Glimpses; or Fifty Years Social, Including Twenty Years Professional Life* (Boston: John P. Jewett and Company, 1856), 304.

First Sunday of Advent

Wanda Burton-Crutchfield

Jeremiah 33:14-16: God will fulfill the promises made to Israel and Judah through one who will be raised up to execute justice and righteousness in the land.

Psalm 25:1-10: The psalmist prays for God's instruction and deliverance.

1 Thessalonians 3:9-13: Paul gives thanks for the Thessalonians and prays that God's love will abide and increase among them.

Luke 21:25-36: Jesus foretells the apocalyptic coming of the Son of Man.

REFLECTIONS

Hope. The word conjures images of violinists strolling through sunlit fields while flowers burst open with the scent of promise. But the lessons of the first Sunday of Advent and the hope they bring assault us like an industrial grunge band screeching in some dank basement. Hope is a challenge. To hope for the coming kingdom of God requires an adventurous spirit, a willingness to risk everything, and a capacity to believe that God's righteousness and justice can prevail.

Throughout chapter 21, the writer of Luke assaults listeners with dire warnings of the destruction of the Temple, national strife, tortured men and women, and cosmic upheaval, all of which climax in a promise. It is then that the Son of Man will return in a cloud of power to redeem them. Jesus promises to return in the world's darkest hour with all the divine glory imaginable. Then the kingdom of God will come on earth as it is in heaven.

But the writer of Luke, addressing the same Gentiles converted and ministered to by Paul,[1] must keep this promise alive even as the first generation of witnesses are dying with cricks in their necks from looking up to an empty sky. Jesus has not come back as quickly as early Christians believed. Luke attempts to stave off the complacency that is likely to set in when humans figure out that God's timetable is not in sync with their own.

It is Luke's warnings in verses 34 through 36 that flavor the sermon that follows. I have long been fascinated with the idea that hope contains a challenge at its core so that it matters what kind of lives we believers live while we wait for the promise of a kingdom of righteousness to come. Our expectations concerning Christ's coming into the world generally sound more like violins than the assault of an electric guitar. Our redemption is near, but are we ready?

A SERMON BRIEF

I was a cereal junkie as a child. Half-eaten boxes of sugary cereals lined the cupboards of my childhood. The boxes of cereal rarely got finished since it was not the cereal I craved. I wanted the toys. It was a brilliant marketing strategist who invented the prize requiring two or more proofs of purchase. I fell for the bait every time. I can still remember the Corn Pops sun catcher requiring three proofs of purchase and a dollar for shipping and handling. Somehow I convinced my mother that the cereal was my sister's favorite as well; multiple-box purchases speed up the process and shorten the wait time. I waited for what seemed an eternity until the long-awaited package arrived. Knowing the importance of the situation, I went to a serene corner of my room near the window soon to be graced by my prize. There I opened the package only to find a two-inch by two-inch tape decal of the company's logo. The prize was not what I expected.

Expectations are a tricky thing. The treasure we seek is rarely the one we find. Expectations in biblical times were a tricky thing as well.

In the passage we read in the Gospel of Luke, Jesus is teaching in the Temple at the end of his earthly ministry. In fact the lesson we read in Luke 21:25-36 is the last such lesson Jesus delivers before he prepares for the Passover celebration he will share with his disciples before his death. With his words, Jesus sketches what is yet to be, what will happen when he returns in glory. An apocalyptical tone falls over the promise of cosmic changes that will leave people fainting and shaken. Jesus encourages his listeners when they see such signs to "stand up and raise your heads, because your redemption is drawing near" (v. 28). Expect the kingdom, Jesus tells those who will hear; it is coming and the old will pass away.

Expectations are a tricky thing. The members of the church in Thessalonica are the proof. Their eyes have been strained, and their necks raised to the sky are cricked by the time Paul writes his letter of encouragement found in 1 Thessalonians. In 1 Thessalonians 3:10, Paul offers a pastoral ear as he croons, "night and day we pray most earnestly that we may see you face to face and restore whatever is lacking in your faith." Jesus has not returned in the timely manner expected. The kingdom of glory promised has not been delivered. The clouds remain empty though the world is full of tumult.

Expectation is a tricky thing, especially when one's stake in the matter does not seem to be paying off. But the writer of Luke, like Paul, knows all too well about expectations and the tricks associated. As only this particular Gospel writer can, the writer of Luke catches his listeners off guard: "Be on guard so that your hearts are not weighed down with dissipation and drunkenness and the worries of this life, and that day does not catch you unexpectedly, like a trap" (21:34-35*a*). Paul packs a similar punch when he says, "may the Lord make you increase and abound in love for one another and for all" (1 Thess. 3:12).

What we do and how we live matters as we wait for the coming kingdom. How we love one another—every person, respectable or not—is at the heart of this faith that God inspires. Our redemption is near. The redemption of the world is at hand. But both must begin in a radical call to live the hope that they are possible. To believe that redemption is possible means that God has made each of us worthy of love, God has called us to live faithfully, and God equips us to live in this new kingdom. When Jesus returns, we have a choice of looking into the sky with joy or hanging our heads in shame.

Expectations are a tricky thing. As we begin a season of waiting for Jesus' coming, for what is it that we hope? We can hope that our comfortable lives in which we are blessed with possessions, luxuries, and excess will go on forever. Or we can hope that God's kingdom rocks our world like a tornado. Surely our redemption is drawing near. It is nothing we expect it to be. Amen.

SUGGESTIONS FOR WORSHIP

Call to Worship (based on Psalm 25:1-10)

ONE: Today, we offer you our lives, O Lord.

MANY: **God, we trust you to take care of us so that those who would laugh at us or consider us foolish for believing in you will know shame, not us.**

ONE: Is that too much to ask when we study, seek your truth, and wait for you?

MANY: **Remember the times in the past when you took care of us just as we ask you to protect us now.**

ONE: What do you think when we try to sweetly blackmail you into doing as we ask rather than live the lives of humility and faith to which you have called us?

MANY: **It should not matter what others say or if we are accepted. You have given us love that does not end and a promise of hope.**

ONE: Today, we offer you our lives, O Lord, no strings attached, just as you offered your life for us all.

Prayer of Confession and Assurance of Pardon

ONE: As we see the flame of hope burning on the altar before us, we should recognize how far from living this hope we are. Enter with me into a time of confession of our sins before God and one another.

ALL: **We are sinners, O Lord. We say we live for the hope of Christ's coming, but we do not. Instead, we have easy chairs and easy lives that keep us on safe streets in pretty places. But you want us to love vagrants and people who think that they are better than us. You would have us fight for justice and live in equity with one another. If hoping your kingdom will come means such upset, we are not sure we want a part of it. Will you forgive us for this doubt lying so quietly at our door? Will you help us to live the redemption that lies in your way? Prepare our hearts for the coming Christ Child. Prepare our hearts for the challenge of hope.**

ONE: Children of hope, know this day that Christ is coming. Christ is coming as a baby who alters everything and is nothing we expect. Christ is coming to redeem us and to give us hope. Accept Christ's gift of forgiveness and of hope.

Benediction

Now may the hope of Christ's coming invade our beings and shake up our world like a cosmic shift. To hope for the not-yet kingdom is to live and love and work and believe that God's redemption changes everything. Look up! The clouds will not be empty forever. Amen.

1. Raymond E. Brown, *An Introduction to the New Testament* (New York: Doubleday, 1997).

Second Sunday of Advent

Jan Fuller Carruthers

Malachi 3:1-4: The prophet Malachi tells of a "messenger of the covenant" who will be sent by God to refine and purify the people.

Luke 1:68-79: Zechariah, the temple priest and father of John the Baptist, foretells the preparatory work of his son and the redemptive work of the one who will follow John.

Philippians 1:3-11: Paul offers thanksgiving for the work of the Philippians and prays that their "love may overflow more and more."

Luke 3:1-6: John preaches a "baptism of repentance for the forgiveness of sins" according to the prophecy of Isaiah who foretold the work of "one crying out in the wilderness."

REFLECTIONS

Malachi, "the Messenger," engages thankless work, confronting distracted people who twist devotion into self-serving efforts. Malachi jabs at their excesses, crying God's hurt and anger for the abuses of devotion, and lament at Israel's faithlessness even after their national deliverance. The people turn away in selfish confusion, confronting God without wanting responses or engagement. They claim to delight in God, yet without respect. They withhold their favors; they cheat on the Beloved. They seek to trade, purchase, and barter divine rewards and blessings in exchange for the image of loyalty.

Both Malachi and John the Baptist call for singular, simple, and selfless devotion, without ambition, without reason. What is hilly, fragmented, and complicated will become simple in response to their questions. Will you love God alone, love God for love's own sake? It

18

is a query for us also. Do we serve God because of what's in it for us—eternal life, salvation, avoidance of punishment, comfort? The truest devotion seeks nothing in return, but welcomes the Beloved, the Most High, into open arms and washed hearts. The messenger shows what steals our affections; what we already carry, hoard, fondle; what we use to build ourselves up, hide behind, or deflect searching light.

A redeemer to come will accomplish purifying salvation. Messengers prepare the way, ready the intended recipients who cannot yet welcome the message. Their arms are full, and their hearts are hard. They must capture the attention of the wholly distracted.

A spiritual seeker traveled, studied, and asked endlessly for life's meaning until she came to the door of a small hut high on a mountain. A sage welcomed her; she talked, wondered, asked, and rebutted. Wisdom brought cup and saucer, pouring. She talked; the sage poured. Tea overflowed the cup, the saucer, splattering to the floor. "Stop!" she cried angrily. "My cup is full!" "Just so," answered the wise one, "Come again when your cup is empty and we'll talk."

A SERMON BRIEF

Sometimes at supper my family plays the Dinner Party game. If you could invite one person—living or dead—to have dinner with us, who would it be? What would you want to talk about? And what would you serve for dinner? We dream of inviting Virginia Woolf, Queen Elizabeth, or Robert Redford. One of the favorite choices is Jesus. Among us we can think of infinite things to talk with him about. While I think we really mean to ask him infinite questions, I wonder if we'll be ready and able to hear him as well.

Somewhere in this lively exchange, I inevitably begin to look around our home. For Queen Elizabeth I'd have to lock the dogs in the basement so they wouldn't lick her legs or beg her scraps. The spare van seat parked along the dining room wall would show up symbolically in a Woolf novel. And for heaven's sake, if Jesus came, I'd really have to clean the place. This latter thought gives me such pause, rather akin to despair, that I attempt to talk the family out of these delightful invitations.

Don't get me wrong. I think housekeeping is a high calling, a respectable profession, one I practice when I'm seized with anxiety, desperation, confusion, or when friends are coming over. (I've also been known to invite people over so we have to straighten.) There's nothing like the presence of an outsider (or even its suggestion) to help us see our own messes, to call chaos to our attention, and to get us moving. The more you unclutter, the more dirt shows and you know how much needs correcting.

Twentieth-century British mystic Evelyn Underhill wrote a lovely little reflection entitled *The House of the Soul* (London: Methuen & Co., 1929). She notes that spiritual life mirrors rather easily the natural or domestic life; the house reflects the spirit of its inhabitant. She visits the soul's lodging, pointing out darkness, light, unexamined storage, decoration, frayed edges, dust. We have infinite ways of hiding the mess; even clever clutter attempts to cover it for others and ourselves. The messenger sees beneath the surface: "Company's coming, and we've got work to do." In any case, I am in serious trouble. We are, too.

Getting ready for Jesus demands our full attention, and we rarely give anything our full attention. Multitasking is the password for survival in our world: e-mail and phone conversations, chores and news radio, prayer and grocery lists, dinner and homework, grading papers at the dentist. It seems we must attain two rewards simultaneously to make an activity worth doing. One isn't enough anymore.

This is the role of the messenger: to capture our wandering attention, to turn our eyes homeward, and to help us perceive what needs clearing, carting away, cleaning, refurbishing. How will our spiritual houses be renewed? Even the question is a sign of hearing the message. We know our distraction, our misappropriation of love, and our selfishness. The great Purifier will do this work, at our invitation; but our focused cooperation is necessary. One thing at a time.

"O Come, O Come, Emmanuel," we sing, perhaps with little intention to really make our homes presentable for such meaningful company. In that case, the Messenger reminds us: get going, take stock, make preparations! Individually and corporately we have to want the purifying, to open ourselves to it, and to commit to faithful pursuit of the goal of loving God with our whole selves. We must give ourselves to this love alone, for its own sake.

Recently I taught a Sunday school class on Islam. A woman interrupted to ask, "Do you mean that they can't pray and iron at the same time?" I love that about Islam. The great confession says that God is one, and means also that only that One matters. Formal prayer has its own focused and uninterrupted time, where only one duty occupies one's full attention. Christians could learn to honor God better through the purity of one thing at a time. Those asking for the

20

presence must prepare for it, ready themselves for the gift of grace, make room for it in the midst of much life-cluttering activity and stuff.

So you want to invite Jesus to your home and heart? Is there room there for another? Is the invitation for you or will it simply honor the Messiah? What needs doing in your heart as you await the Messiah? Is the way prepared, straight and smooth, and free of damaging distractions?

A jeweler traveled to study with a Chinese jade master. On the first day of training the master blindfolded him, put a stone in his hand, said, "This is jade," and departed. At the end of the day, he wordlessly took the stone and removed the blindfold. The next day the master blindfolded him, put a stone in his hand. "This is jade." The days, weeks, months went by. One day the master placed a stone in his hand, and the blindfolded student burst out, "I came to learn jade from you, the Master who knows so much. For months you simply set stones in my hand in darkness. I have had enough! And today— of all days—this stone is not even jade!" The master removed the blindfold and, smiling, said, "Your lessons are done. You may go now."

The Messengers call the community to one thing—the truest of loves in relation to the Holy One and to one another. We know it fully by training, by exposure to it, in the simplicity of its practice. Unlike the student of jade, we never finish mastering this love. But we make ready again and again, for the coming of the Christ, Love Incarnate in our world, in our hearts. The messenger cries, "Prepare the way of the Lord, make the paths straight." May it be so.

SUGGESTIONS FOR WORSHIP

Call to Worship (from Philippians 1:3-11)

In this place, in these approaching moments, only one thing is required of us. Rest, rest, rest in God's love. There is room here for all you are, all you bring, every concern and joy. Hear the Holy Voice say, "Come." Hear the awesome stillness. Open your heart to it, and worship the God of tender mercy who began a good work in you and will bring it to completion at the day of Jesus Christ. Come. Rest.

Prayer of Confession (from Luke 1:68-79)

ONE: Let us confess our hearts and lives before God and one another.

ALL: **God of compassion, we are not nearly ready to welcome you. Our preparations are late and inadequate, our hearts are distracted by worries, hopes, and material clutter. We are a disorderly people. We do not yet love justice and mercy, we do not yet seek peace, so we cannot walk as friends with you. We are sinners. Come to us, O Holy and Tender One, to forgive us and save us.**

ONE: Through the tender mercy of our God, the day dawns upon us from on high. God gives light to us who sat in darkness and death. God saves us, forgives us, and sends us forth from this moment on, to live as new people. Amen.

Third Sunday of Advent

Dawn Darwin Weaks

Zephaniah 3:14-20: After expressing God's fierce judgment upon all the earth, the prophet speaks words of reassurance that God will restore God's people despite their faithlessness.

Isaiah 12:2-6: The prophet acts as a worship leader to prompt the people's songs of praise in thanks to God for their deliverance.

Philippians 4:4-7: Even from a prison cell, Paul's instructions speak of joy, gentleness, and peace available to the believer in Christ.

Luke 3:7-18: John the Baptist preaches good news to the crowds, exhorting them to live penitent, justice-oriented lives in preparation for the Messiah's coming.

REFLECTIONS

"Joy" is the traditional third Sunday of Advent theme in many churches. In contrast to purple, a rose candle is often used in the Advent wreath on this Sunday, a hue that imitates the lighting up of the skies just before day breaks. This is the function of our readings. Each speaks of joy—joy after judgment in the prophets, joy in the midst of trial in Philippians, and even "good news" somehow found in the words of challenge spoken by John the Baptist. How is true joy possible in each of these settings, where darkness lingers and day has not yet come?

Zephaniah points to a clear source of our joy as his recorded words draw to a close. Though he has issued stinging indictments of the political and religious leaders of the people, though he has thoroughly warned the people of God's hot anger, he now speaks good

23

news. The people apparently are beyond self-improvement. God will come into their midst. God will free them from oppression. God will remove their iniquities. God will gather them together again and lead them home. God plans to sing loudly and proudly over the people one day, as a warrior sings proudly over his victory, as a mother sings proudly over her children. We have joy because our deliverance is not entirely up to us.

A SERMON BRIEF

God Sings

Are you ready for a merry Christmas? For many folk, a "merry" Christmas seems far out of reach. We don't always acknowledge it, but many people are weighed down by unhappiness at this time of year. Some are grieving the death of a loved one, some are battling depression or addiction, some are entangled in painful family dynamics, and some are weary with illness. Some are worried about looming problems on the global scene. Some haven't paid much attention to God in a long time and resent the reminders of God's presence around every decorated corner. Some feel like God couldn't care less. Indeed, a lot of folk aren't too joyful. And to be honest, can we blame them? Can we even acknowledge the true difficulties in our own lives with "Joy to the World" sung every time we turn on the radio?

The prophet Zephaniah wrote to a people weighed down in the aftermath of the oppression of the Assyrian empire. Their political and religious leaders had bowed to foreign leaders and foreign gods. The poor and the outcast were ignored while people pursued worldly wealth. Corruption and violence ran rampant from the courthouse to the sanctuary. The people grew so weary of the moral stench and spiritual vacuum in which they lived that they had become indifferent to God. They didn't think God could make a difference in their lives— not in their grief, their poverty, their fear, or their shame.

God called Zephaniah to speak a word from the Lord to these ancestors of our faith who had lost their trust in God. Yet the first two and a half chapters of the book of Zephaniah hardly sound like words of comfort to a people in captivity. Zephaniah speaks harshly on behalf of the Lord, especially admonishing the leaders for their waywardness and their lack of trust in God. God is fiercely angry, Zephaniah warns. God will consume the earth in the fires of his passion (1:18). The great day of the Lord is coming. Instead of "Joy to the World," Zephaniah sings "Wrath to the World," the Lord is coming!

But wait. Something changes. God relents. Zephaniah ceases words of warning and destruction and gives birth to new hope with words of comfort. Maybe God remembers that we humans cannot restore ourselves on our own; perhaps God's parental heart breaks at the thought of continuing to punish these precious children. Regardless, Zephaniah stops telling the people what they've done wrong and starts telling them what God is doing right. "Rejoice!" Zephaniah says. "Look what God is going to do for you! Your judgment has been taken away. God is with you! You don't have to be afraid anymore. God is victorious over all of your enemies. And God will sing a song of rejoicing over you!"

Then—another change—the text shifts from Zephaniah speaking for God to God speaking for God's own self! Zephaniah has told us there would be a song, and God begins singing it! "I will save you," God sings to the people, "I will help the lame and the outcast, and I will lift up those who are ashamed. I will bring you home and give you everything you need!" The voice of God lifts off the printed page and becomes a resounding love song for all to hear. It turns out that God yearns for joy, too, and is willing to step in and do for us what we cannot do for ourselves so that we can live in joy.

A few years ago I was visiting a member of my congregation at the Veterans Administration hospital. I was waiting with him in a patient holding area, where many others were waiting for various tests and procedures. Our visit was interrupted by the sound of a man groaning loudly and the softer sound of a woman humming. As the noise continued, I excused myself from our visit and followed the sound of the groaning and the singing. I turned the corner to see a badly scarred man lying on a gurney, groaning and speaking non-sensically. Beside him sat a woman, stroking his brow and humming gently to him. I introduced myself and asked if I could sit with them for a few moments. The woman seemed glad for the company. She told me their story. He had been wounded in Vietnam, resulting in severe mental and physical handicaps. "He's been like this ever since," she ended. My mind raced to do the math—for thirty years they had suffered like this. I was speechless. Finally, I asked, perhaps selfishly, "If you don't mind me asking, how have you endured?" She smiled and said, "I know that one day God's gonna come and heal him. And I intend to be here when he does." And she began humming again.

I'm not sure, but I think that in the sound of her humming song, I heard the sound of God singing, too. She was humming the tune that fits the promise we find here in Zephaniah. It was just the beginning, but it was a hint of the loud love song to come. It was the first bars of a ballad of boisterous victory over sin and disease and oppression and all that keeps us from joy. It was the lullaby of a mother comforting her child; it was the raucous tune of a warrior when he has won the battle. I'm not sure, but I think that in the sound of her humming song, I heard the sound of God singing, too.

Perhaps then "Joy to the World" is not the song for those of us who cannot find much joy this time of year. Perhaps "It Came Upon a Midnight Clear" is a more genuine expression of our faith. This Advent, you who are "beneath life's crushing load," "rest beside the weary road, and hear"—not just the angels singing—but our great God Almighty, singing over you.

SUGGESTIONS FOR WORSHIP

Call to Worship (based on Isaiah 12:2-6)

LEADER: Come, give thanks to the Lord; call on God's name. Let every nation know the mighty deeds of our God!
PEOPLE: Surely God is our salvation.
LEADER: People of God, the Holy One is in your midst.
PEOPLE: Let us sing praises to the Lord. Let us shout aloud and sing for joy!

Pastoral Prayer

O God, you are our deliverer and our salvation. We give thanks this day that you are not deterred from coming to our aid by our indifference or our lack of trust in you. Though we have ignored you and turned our trust to lesser gods, you have never given up on us. We acknowledge in these quiet moments that you are the one true God, and we yearn to be your faithful people once again. Restore to us the joy of our salvation. Help us, O God, to turn to you more quickly when we are afraid and to rely on you more fully when we have decisions to make. Give courage to those who fight against temptation. Give relief to those who bear the burden of grief. Give hope to those who struggle with illness. Give reassurance to those who doubt you.

Prepare us by your Holy Spirit to receive the gift of Jesus Christ, our Savior, once more. Amen.

Benediction (based on Philippians 4:4-7)

Rejoice in the Lord. Let God carry the burdens of your heart. And the peace of God, which surpasses all understanding, will guard your hearts and minds in Christ Jesus. Rejoice in the Lord!

Fourth Sunday of Advent

Judith FaGalde Bennett

Micah 5:2-5a: The prophet proclaims a peaceful ruler who will come from Bethlehem.

Luke 1:47-55: Mary sings a song of praise.

Psalm 80:1-7: Israel beseeches God for salvation and restoration.

Hebrews 10:5-10: We have been sanctified through Christ, the ultimate sacrifice.

Luke 1:39-45 (46-55): Mary visits Elizabeth and receives her blessing.

REFLECTIONS

Protestants are only beginning to understand and appreciate Mary and the role she can play in our faith, whether by balancing male imagery of God or by offering an example of faithful obedience. As a woman, I have always hungered for both. As a Christian woman, I revel in the work of women scholars who make accessible the stories of women in the pages of Scripture. I have especially loved the stories of Elizabeth and Mary and their improbable pregnancies. Also, as one who has long been fascinated by other cultures, I rejoice when I find a scholar who sheds light on the cultural world of the Bible, placing biblical figures in the context of their everyday world.

One such scholar, John J. Pilch, points out that it would have been very odd indeed for Mary to have made such a journey alone, especially given her youth and her pregnancy, for "women in the ancient Middle East could never do anything alone" but had to be "always in a cluster of women and children or under the watchful eye of their father, brother, husband, or some other responsible male relative."[1] Further, Pilch suggests, she would not so soon have headed home, because only an "unfeeling kinswoman" would "leave Elizabeth at the moment of her greatest need, childbirth!"[2] But, no matter, says Pilch; it's a wonderful faith-filled "true" story, making the point that "God does indeed work in strange and mysterious ways."[3]

Surely, Mary must have been a remarkable woman or she would not have been remembered in such a way. To see her as a woman of deep faith, to hear her speak for the lowly as she sings her song of ancient promises and coming liberation, is to discover a mother in the faith who can challenge women and men in our own time. It is also to expand our understanding of the God who would come to be born of a woman, to put on our flesh and walk among us, challenging us to work for justice and peace in our world.

A SERMON BRIEF

Remembering Mary

My understanding of Mary is different from that of most Protestants, I suspect, perhaps because I didn't grow up in the church. I was in and out of many churches, but it was not until I was a teenager that I found community in a downtown United Methodist congregation. Between my troubled family and the tough neighborhood in which we lived, the sole respite I remember in my stress-filled childhood was the few months I attended Ascension School, a Catholic school near our home.

I was there on our doctor's recommendation. Neighborhood bullies made the long walk to public school like running the gauntlet for a small-for-her-age six-year-old, and the ordeal was affecting my health. The nuns ran a tight ship, where bullying was not tolerated. There were rules, to be sure, but there was also love. Each morning at mass my head should have been covered, but most days my mother forgot. Sister Rosouitha, ever patient and ever hopeful of the eventual salvation of my soul, pulled from the folds of her habit a large white handkerchief, neatly ironed into a small square. With a snap of her wrist the handkerchief came to full attention, revealing itself as an arrangement of many squares, and was securely knotted under my chin. This was the part of the day I loved best. Unfortunately, pressure from anti-Catholic grandparents soon led to my removal from Ascension. On my final day there, Sister Rosouitha knelt beside me on the playground, put her arms around me and said, "Don't ever forget the Baby Jesus and the Blessed Mother." I promised her I would not forget them.

Later, in third grade, with two younger siblings to shepherd to and from school each day, I was charged with their safety—a daunting task, indeed. Two things got me through. First, I could kick like a mule. I discovered that if I kept my wits about me and let an approaching bully come in very close, I could deliver the swift and incapacitating kick; and we could run like the wind all the way home, while our attacker howled in pain. Second, I remembered Sister Rosouitha and the Blessed Mother, imagining the strong arms of either or both wrapping me in safety and love, and my heart stayed calm—more or less!

As Protestants, we have missed a sense of Mary as a presence. The passage from Luke's Gospel helps us to glimpse her humility, her strength, her obedient discipleship, and her passion for justice. Indeed, Mary's joyful song of response to Elizabeth's testimony can be considered the first preaching of the good news in Luke's Gospel as she sings of what God is doing.

Virtually every line of her song echoes the Hebrew Scriptures that were in her spiritual DNA. One more time, God is doing a new and unexpected thing, but the God of surprises is still the faithful God of times past—consistent and continuous and ever to be trusted. Now, in the child to be born, God will move among God's chosen people. But who are these people, and where do we find them? They are not the mighty, nor the proud. They are not found among the priests of the temple or on the thrones of mighty empires. They are the poor, the lowly, and the insignificant folk of the backwaters of the ancient world. And a lowly woman, young and unmarried, will bear a child; and all generations will call her blessed. Her heart overflows in joyous praise, and her song describes the world that will be—the world that already is. In Mary's song, God has *already* accomplished what is to be; we need only recognize it and begin to live our lives accordingly. Luke's Gospel tells an amazing story of a world turned upside down, and we glimpse the dimensions of that inversion in Mary's song.

But what will this upside-down world look like? How will we recognize it? There are exciting new voices among students of the Bible in our time, who focus on the Gospels to unpack that vision for us in challenging ways. Ched Myers writes that the new thing God is doing will not be a repeat of "the weary old story of the world, in which the powers always win and the poor always lose,"[4] but will be radically revised. All will be different because the child Mary bears will challenge the political and religious authority of this world, moving among them with an altogether different kind of authority.

The source of that authority is love—love that is deep enough, strong enough to overcome evil. Most of us like to think of ourselves as being loving people, persons who are opposed to evil; but the problem for most of us is that in the process of opposing evil, we become like the evil we oppose. As we look at our world, the angels' message about peace on earth becomes a poignant reminder of our failure. Loving in the face of evil is frightening and costly. Even so, Walter Wink sees many signs in our time of persons and movements—like Gandhi in India and Martin Luther King, Jr., in this country—that have achieved great individual and social change by shunning violence and continuing to love. If we are honest, Wink writes, when we look at the record of violence all around us, we can see that Jesus' way "is the only way to overcome evil without creating new forms of evil and making us evil in turn."[5]

Are we ready for Christmas? Are we ready for the arrival of *this* Baby, the one who will grow to be a man who will turn the world upside down? Mary sings of the God who is her Savior, the God-who-is-doing-a-new-thing—the same God who is at work in our world and who is *our* Savior, wrapping strong arms of love around the mess we have made of our world, putting the broken pieces of our lives back together again. This God is not some divine hand reaching down from the heavenly places to put bandages on our wounded lives, but the God who reaches out to us through the very human arms of other persons, imperfect persons like Gandhi and King and Sister Rosouitha and you and me. This is the gift we can give one another.

Joy to the world; the Lord is come!

SUGGESTIONS FOR WORSHIP

Call to Worship (adapted from Micah 5:2-5*a*)

LEADER:	Our God comes to us as a baby in a manger.
PEOPLE:	**Our God comes as a shepherd to feed the flock.**
LEADER:	The shepherd will stand in the strength of our God,
PEOPLE:	**And the name of the shepherd is Love.**
LEADER:	The child shall be great to the ends of the earth,
PEOPLE:	**And the name of the child is Peace.**

Benediction (adapted from Luke 1:46-55)

Go now to await the birth of the Holy Child, whose mercy is for those who fear him from generation to generation. Find ways in this season to lift up the lowly and fill the hungry with good things. And let *your* soul magnify the Lord and *your* spirit rejoice in God our Savior. Go in peace. Amen.

1. John J. Pilch, *The Cultural World of Jesus: Sunday by Sunday, Cycle C* (Collegeville, Minn.: The Liturgical Press, 1997), 10.

2. Ibid., 12.

3. Ibid.

4. Ched Myers, et al. *Say to This Mountain: Mark's Story of Discipleship* (Maryknoll, N.Y.: Orbis Books, 1996), 209.

5. Walter Wink, *The Powers That Be: Theology for a New Millennium* (New York: Doubleday, 1998), 127.

Christmas Eve

Teresa Lockhart Stricklen

Isaiah 9:2-7: Isaiah prophesies the coming of light upon those who have lived in darkness by means of the gift of a child who will be a mighty and righteous ruler.

Psalm 96: The psalmist declares God's glory as well as the coming of God's righteous judgment upon the earth.

Titus 2:11-14: Jesus Christ is proclaimed as the manifestation of God and the means of salvation and grace.

Luke 2:1-14 (15-20): Jesus is born to Mary and Joseph in Bethlehem, heralded by angels and visited by shepherds.

REFLECTIONS

This sermon is written for a rowdy Christmas Eve church service with all sorts of folk showing up—one different from the holiness of the midnight mass tradition. If you are doing a quiet service, Psalm 96 can figure prominently in the meditation. But for the family of God service, the old, old story is one that never grows old and as such serves as the basis for this meditation. The sermon is brief, part of a whole service where the liturgy is designed to preach as much as the sermon to draw us all together around the manger. Though the text for the sermon is ostensibly Luke 2, the broader nativity story is brought in partly as incentive to read the other stories besides just the one we hear all the time. Psalm 96:3 also figures in the hermeneutic orientation of God's "marvelous works among all the peoples." It was all the different kinds of people from all walks of life gathered together in Luke's nativity story around a baby born out among the animals that served as the elements for the following meditation.

A SERMON BRIEF

One church had two Christmas Eve services. One service started at 11 P.M. with only a faithful few. It was quiet, with deep, dark, ponderous silence, reflective liturgy that matched the plethora of candles, and Holy Communion from silver. You could almost hear angels singing across the windswept "Silent Night." The church's other Christmas Eve service began at 7 P.M. with lots of rowdy children scrambling everywhere in a flurry of velvet dresses and bow ties being chased by weary parents in casual pants and bright Christmas sweaters. Though we sang "Silent Night" during the candle lighting ceremony at the end, it was hardly silent. It was a zoo.

Though there's a part of us that craves the deep reflective silence of the 11:00 service, the 7:00 service is probably more faithful to Luke's story of Jesus' nativity where we have a cast of characters that makes Jesus' birth look like a zoo.

Consider the familiar story again. What a strange group of characters Luke presents to us. Look at all the different species of humankind roaming through Luke's Gospel like different animals in a modern-day zoo wandering through a common savannah. Luke's Gospel opens with the ubiquitous secular powers roaring in the background. "In the days of King Herod," "a decree went out from Emperor Augustus," "while Quirinius was governor." It's as though Luke is warning us to never forget that in the background of this story lions of power lie in wait. But there's another often overlooked character in the cast of nameless crowds of people praying and hoping for deliverance: a crowd that roams as prolific through Luke's Gospel as antelope mulling about on the savannah. Then there's Zechariah, a priest doing Temple duty as one of the religious elite, steady as an elephant, a well-respected member of his community whom everyone knew, kind of like a pastor of a small town. Then we have Zechariah's wife Elizabeth, the blue-blood daughter of a priest, who with God's help gets pregnant at last with John the Baptist, a character who leaps into Luke's Gospel like the wild man of the jungle, looking as wild and woolly as a gorilla. Then along strolls Mary like a beautiful giraffe, a young girl who says to God's wild proposition, "Let it be with me according to your word," despite the fact that under the law she should be put to death for being with child by someone other than her betrothed Joseph. And Joseph! Good ol' "just Joe" cheated out of his lovely bride who nonetheless saves and protects her, a man who doesn't see things as black and white as a zebra but one who understands the nature of God's law as based upon mercy. Then there are the scruffy shepherds who show up after the birth of the child, veritable jackals, hardened folk with a reputation for criminal activity. Shepherds were marginal people—poor, down-on-their-luck, children put to work early. Yet can't you see them—grizzle-faced, gently holding the baby, wide brown-toothed grins that match the smiles of everyone else who takes up a baby in this story.

So many different human characters all gathered around the most common human element—a baby, the baby Jesus. And that's just the cast of *human* characters in Luke's nativity story—not to mention the all-powerful God who steals the show or the angels hovering over everything like a morning mist rising from an earth being transformed by good news of God's new work, singing "Glory to God in the highest!" My goodness, so many different folk! Were they not frozen like little statues in our romantic nativity scenes, these different species of folk wouldn't get along for more than fifteen minutes. So many different characters; it's a zoo.

Maybe that's the point, God's ludicrous point—a baby born right in the middle of this zoo called humanity. For in the center of all is a bawling baby filled with God's Spirit who came to clean up the elephant-house stench of sin that we live in so that all God's creatures could live in harmony as intended without the need for bars between us. When you think about it, being born in a manger among the animals is an apt description of God acting in our human situation structured by the sin of a dog-eat-dog world to transform it into one in which a lamb can sleep peacefully with a wolf instead of ending up as dinner. So now instead of devouring one another, with the coming of the Christ Child, we can serve one another the feast of God's new creation born with Christ our paschal lamb, splayed out in all the vulnerability of a newborn baby whose innocent death on the political cross of lions forces us to look upon the mess we've made of this thing called life, to take responsibility for our sin forgiven by the power of God, and to be transformed through the working of God's Spirit Way. Maybe that's the point of this zoo-like configuration of characters: God at work among the animals. [Moving to communion table with nativity scene in front.] God gathering the whole of a rowdy, raucous humanity around an innocent babe in a feeding trough.

SUGGESTIONS FOR WORSHIP

Call to Worship (based on Isaiah 9:2-7)

LEADER: The people who walked in darkness have seen a great light; those who lived in a land of deep darkness—on them light has shined.

PEOPLE: **You have multiplied the nation, you have increased its joy; they rejoice before you as with joy at the harvest, as people exult when dividing plunder.**

LEADER: For a child has been born for us, a son has been given to us;

PEOPLE: **And he is named Wonderful Counselor, Mighty God, Everlasting Father, Prince of Peace.** [Move to the lighting of the Christ candle on the Advent wreath.]

Prayer of Adoration and Confession

Holy Child, born of Mary in a barn, you identify with us in abject humanity. You move among us with announcements of good news when things look bleak; you give us a star on dark, lonely nights. Sing to us once more that, assured of your presence among us, we may forget our fear and embrace your gift of newborn life, to the glory of your holy name we pray. Amen.

Invitation to Holy Communion

So come, let all us different folk adore him. Good religious folks, scruffy shepherds, blue-bloods, young women, good ol' Joes, children, seekers after truth, come. Bring your bulletins and your candles, and let's gather around the newborn babe. Help one another as needed (for those who have difficulty walking). Those of you who cannot stand can sit on the outside edge of the pew—whatever works. But let the circle be unbroken. Come, let us adore Emmanuel.

("O Come All Ye Faithful" can be sung as people gather in a large circle that encompasses the sanctuary's perimeter.)

Benediction (from Isaiah 9:2 and 60:1)

The people who walked in darkness have seen a great light; those who lived in a land of deep darkness—on them light has shined. (The pastor lights her candle from the Christ candle, then passes it around the circle with all singing an appropriate hymn.) Arise, shine; for your light has come, and the glory of the Lord has risen upon you. (Close by singing "Joy to the World.")

Epiphany of the Lord

Amy Louise Na

Isaiah 60:1-6: In a dark world where hope seems distant, the prophet calls God's people to embrace the light, the glory, and the blessings that God shall provide.

Psalm 72:1-7, 10-14: This psalm is a prayer to God on behalf of the king. When the king is blessed, so are his people.

Ephesians 3:1-12: In some detail, Paul outlines the mission to which he was called, that of bringing the gospel to the Gentiles for God's eternal purposes.

Matthew 2:1-12: Wise men consult with the king, follow a star, find Jesus and worship him. They return to their country avoiding King Herod so that Herod never learns of Jesus' exact location.

REFLECTIONS

The Gospel text is a great text because it rounds out our Christmas celebrations and makes our manger scene complete. Matthew is the only gospel writer who includes this story about the Magi. The text is filled with stars, secrets, plots, and predictions. Upon their arrival in Jerusalem, the wise men, probably from a Persian priestly caste, inquire about the one born king of the Jews. Fearful for himself and his offspring, King Herod learns from the local chief priests of Jesus' birth in Bethlehem. Herod secretly consults with the Magi before they follow the star, which stopped over the place where Jesus was. A dream warns the wise men to avoid the king and to return home another way. Their secret visit and Herod's insecurity precedes the bitter text of the innocents slaughtered in Herod's attempt to control the future of his kingdom and to thwart God's plan for the one born king of the Jews.

The text is rich with prophecy and human calculation among other themes. But the secret meetings and the hidden travel plans in contrast to the bright star in the sky exposes the powerful presence of an abiding God. Notwithstanding all the human efforts to control Jesus' entrance and early survival, God prevails. God, in Christ, comes to earth and reveals in great and small ways and according to plan God's desire to be known to God's people.

A SERMON BRIEF

Star light, star bright . . .

One of the first things beyond our home and family that my son liked was stars. He was fascinated with them. We looked at night for patterns and falling stars. He struggled with small fingers and two-year-old coordination to draw a five-pointed star. We purchased glow-in-the-dark plastic ones for the walls and ceiling of his room. One birthday brought five star lights in a sparkling set from his Gram that lit up his nighttime walls all winter long. To him, stars were light and beauty and mystery all at once.

His fascination with stars may be compared to that of the Magi in the Gospel text for today. They were astrologers, students of the stars. They first came to inquire about Jesus because they observed his star at its rising. In secret meetings with Herod, they could describe the exact time when the star appeared. They followed the same star until it stopped over the place where Jesus was. Jesus' birth stirred a star, a search party, and a king. His birth was the light to life for a dark world, and the star over him proclaimed such a message.

God's message of love and forgiveness, of covenant and salvation is one of old. Since Adam, God has chosen to be revealed to humanity. In the history of the Bible, God has been revealed, but always only partially and oftentimes in the presence of light. With Moses, God's self-revelation occurred in the fire; the bush burned, but it was not consumed. God was a piercing, hot light. On the mountain, God caused Moses' face to shine; then Moses wore a veil to cover—partially—God's brightness. The light of the star, visible only by night, caused the magi to visit the place where the Messiah was born. The king of the Jews had come to earth, as a newborn baby. God is revealed, but only partially. In the Gospel of Mark, at Jesus' death, the curtain of the Temple was torn in two (Mark 15:38). Curtains block sunlight. The tearing of the curtain or veil covering the Temple brought to light the mystery of God in Christ through his death. In light and power, in death and in quiet, God has been revealed to God's people.

In these days we celebrate God's revelation in Christ. We celebrate the season with light. We celebrate with candles and twinkling lights and bright trees inside and outside our homes. There are lights decorating neighborhoods and businesses proclaiming a season of joy and hope. The light brightens the night and dispels some of the darkness in our lives. Light exposes. Light reveals. Light announces. Light demands. One such light is a star.

In light and in dreams, God is revealed to us. When the Christmas lights are put away, God's light remains. The sun, the moon, and all the stars stay in the sky. They are fixed and dependable; they are there to light our way. They can serve as a reminder of the constant presence of Almighty God in the midst of sickness, confusion, turmoil, doubt, and fear.

In these days, we celebrate light and we sing about stars in the sky: silent ones looking down on the manger, the place where Jesus lay. In Jesus' birth, God is exposed and revealed, announced and even demanding, as only a baby can be. In these days, we celebrate the knowledge and the thrill of Jesus' birth. A star reminds us of all this.

"Star light, star bright, first star I see tonight . . ." are the words to a popular children's rhyme. My son and I say it when we look at the stars at night. Stars are little night lights, surrounding us. On your many errands and busy evening events, take time to look up at the stars. Make a wish. Remember the holy birth. Let the light of even the tiniest star give you hope in a dark world. The star, the little light suspended in the darkness shines, and its brilliance, whether small or large, is constant. It is as though God is saying to us: *I am here. I am with you. I will lead the way. I have come so that you will know me. You are not alone.*

May the star light remind you of the Light of the world. May the mystery and the light of this season bring you closer to the Lord of all, the Light of life.

SUGGESTIONS FOR WORSHIP

Call to Worship (based on Isaiah 60)

LEADER: In a world where silence and darkness linger . . .
PEOPLE: Arise, shine, for the light has come.

LEADER:	In a world where sadness and fear remain . . .
PEOPLE:	**The glory of the Lord has risen upon us.**
LEADER:	Let the nations and peoples, our sons and daughters, gather together,
PEOPLE:	**Rejoice and give thanks for the abundance around us.**
ALL:	**Let us be radiant; let our hearts thrill and rejoice. Let us proclaim the incarnate Christ, the light of all. Let us worship God.**

Prayer of Confession/ Assurance of Pardon (based on Ephesians 3:1-12)

LEADER:	With full and contrite hearts, let us bow our heads and confess our sins together. Let us pray.
ALL:	**Gracious God, who gave us your son, our Savior, you shine upon us and bless and increase our lives. Yet we fail to follow your ways. We neglect your message and its saving grace for ourselves, and we doubt it for our neighbors. Teach us your mysteries and help us to forgive, as you forgive us. We pray through Jesus Christ our Lord. Amen.**
LEADER:	Sisters and brothers, children of God, hear and believe that the mystery of God's grace and the promise of God's forgiveness are for you. In accordance with God's eternal plan in Jesus Christ, we are forgiven. Amen. Thanks be to God.

Benediction

Jesus said, "I am the light of the world. Whoever follows me will not walk in darkness, but will have the light of life." May the light of the Messiah guide you through the dark and the mystery of this day and every day. Amen.

41

Baptism of the Lord

Marsha M. Wilfong

Isaiah 43:1-7: God will redeem all who are called by God's name, promising deliverance when they pass through waters and fire.

Psalm 29: The "voice of the Lord" is heard in a thunderstorm, revealing God's power and glory.

Acts 8:14-17: After the people of Samaria had been baptized by Philip in the name of the Lord Jesus, they received the Holy Spirit as Peter and John laid hands upon them.

Luke 3:15-17, 21-22: John proclaims the difference between himself and the Messiah to come. Jesus also is baptized, and while he is praying, the heaven opened, the Spirit descended upon him, and a voice from heaven spoke.

REFLECTIONS

The Gospel text is the Lukan account of Jesus' baptism. This lection has two parts. In the first part, verses 15-17, John declares the difference between his baptism, "with water," and that of the Messiah to come, "with the Holy Spirit and fire" (v. 16). In the second part, verses 21-22, Jesus' own baptism is both connected with other baptisms (v. 21a) and distinguished from them by the descent of the Holy Spirit and the voice from heaven (vv. 21b-22).

Implicit in the text is the question of our baptism as Christians. Christian baptism involves the Holy Spirit and fire. But what does "fire" signify? Verse 17 speaks of the "fire" of judgment: The wheat will be gathered, but the chaff will be burned "with unquenchable fire." However, the story of Pentecost in Acts 2:1-4 connects the Holy Spirit and fire in a different way. The tongues of fire are a visible sign of the outpouring of the Holy Spirit on the disciples. The Old Testament lection, Isaiah 43:1-7, promises deliverance from fire (and water): "when you walk through fire you shall not be burned, and the flame shall not consume you" (Isa. 43:2*b*). Thus, it appears that the fire associated with baptism is a "refining fire," a burning away of the impurities (or "chaff") within the baptized—a dying to sin, in the process of rising to new life in Christ.

This sermon focuses on the work of the Holy Spirit in Jesus' baptism and in our own. It draws on the ongoing activity of the Holy Spirit in Jesus' life in the fourth chapter of Luke to help hearers make a connection between the event of Christian baptism and the living out of Christian life.

A SERMON BRIEF

The Holy Spirit is something we hear about a lot in the church. We read about the Holy Spirit in Scripture. We confess our faith in God the Holy Spirit, along with God the Father and God the Son. Some of us even talk about the ways in which the Holy Spirit has been active in our lives—or at least acknowledge that we long for the Spirit's guidance. Yet for many Christians, the Holy Spirit remains a mystery— something we *claim* to believe in, but something that remains difficult to understand. One place to begin unraveling the mystery is to look at the work of the Holy Spirit in the life of Jesus. Perhaps then we can better understand the Spirit's activity in our own.

The first mention of the Holy Spirit in Jesus' life is at the moment of conception. Through the creative power of God's Holy Spirit, Mary conceived and bore a child who was both human and the Son of God. The next mention of the Holy Spirit in Jesus' life is at his baptism. And that's where we come into the picture. Because for us, *baptism* is the point at which, through the power of the Holy Spirit, *we* are reborn as children of God.

So what happened at Jesus' baptism? What part did the Holy Spirit play? What difference did it make in Jesus' life?

According to Luke's Gospel, Jesus came to be baptized along with many other people who responded to John's call to repentance. But after Jesus' baptism, while he was praying, "the heaven was opened, and the Holy Spirit descended upon him. . . . And a voice came from heaven, 'You are my Son, the Beloved; with you I am well pleased.' " That's not a very detailed description! And yet, it tells us a lot. It tells

43

us that baptism is not a magical act through which we are automatically in communion with God. Rather, baptism opens the way for us to come to God in prayer. As we open ourselves up to God, bringing to God our needs and failures, our desires and hopes, God becomes more accessible to us.

Jesus was praying—and "the heaven was opened." God who seemed hidden became visible and real. Jesus was praying—"and the Holy Spirit descended upon him. . . ." God who seemed distant came near: God's presence was felt in every fiber of Jesus' being. Jesus was praying—"and a voice came down from heaven." God who seemed silent was revealed as a loving parent who delights in the very existence of his or her child.

Such is the work of the Holy Spirit in our lives, too—not just at the moment of our baptism, but whenever we claim the promises of our baptism and turn to God in prayer. The Holy Spirit makes God visible when God seems hidden, assures us of God's presence when God seems distant, and reveals God's love for us as God's children. All of us have moments when God is so real and so near, when we feel God's love all around us, when we feel God's power uplifting us, when we know that we belong to God in a special way. It's as if we are home at last, at peace with God, with ourselves, with the world around us. We wish that those moments would last forever. But they don't.

And neither did that moment at Jesus' baptism. That's because creating a sense of communion with God is not the only work of the Holy Spirit. In moments of intense communion with God, the Spirit is also preparing us for something more.

If we read on in the fourth chapter of Luke's Gospel, we discover two other aspects of the Spirit's work. The chapter begins with these words: "Jesus, full of the Holy Spirit, returned from the Jordan and was led by the Spirit in the wilderness, where for forty days he was tempted by the devil." It is comforting to note that God's Spirit was present with Jesus in the midst of temptation. It is troubling, however, to realize that the Spirit also *led* him to the place of temptation. Why would a loving God do that?

That is often our question in the face of temptation. Yet, sometimes we *need* to be led into confrontation with the things that tempt us. Otherwise, we may never realize just how much things such as power or wealth or popularity or security mean to us. Until we know what it is we would be willing to sell out God in order to possess or be, we cannot resist the temptation. Until we face whatever tempts

44

us, we cannot know the full strength that the Holy Spirit offers to aid our resistance. Being driven into temptation may seem like a harsh test. But it is also a revelation. Through such experiences, the Holy Spirit reveals to us our weakness, but also the limitlessness of God's power and love. Only when we know that can God's strength overcome our weakness.

When Jesus returned from the wilderness, he went to the synagogue in Nazareth, where he preached his first sermon. The text was from the prophet Isaiah:

"The Spirit of the Lord is upon me,
   because he has anointed me to bring good news to the poor.
He has sent me to proclaim release to the captives
   and recovery of sight to the blind,
   to let the oppressed go free.
to proclaim the year of the Lord's favor." (Luke 4:18-19)

That day in Nazareth, this text was not just a reading from Isaiah, but a declaration of Jesus' vocation. For the Holy Spirit not only drove Jesus to face temptation, it also drove him to ministry, to proclaim and carry out God's own work.

Neither Jesus nor we received God's Holy Spirit to *have* as our possession. We, like Jesus, receive the Holy Spirit in order to minister to others—so that they too may know the joy of communion with God, so that they too may gain the power to resist temptation, so that they too may have good news to preach.

SUGGESTIONS FOR WORSHIP

Call to Worship (from Psalm 29:10-11)

LEADER: The LORD sits enthroned over the flood;
            the LORD sits enthroned as king forever.
PEOPLE: **May the LORD give strength to his people!**
            May the LORD bless his people with peace!

Assurance of Pardon (Isaiah 43:1, 3*a*)

But now thus says the LORD,
   he who created you, O Jacob,

45

he who formed you, O Israel:
Do not fear, for I have redeemed you;
   I have called you by name, you are mine.
 For I am the LORD your God,
   the Holy One of Israel, your Savior.

Friends, the good news is that God has fulfilled this promise. In Jesus Christ you have been redeemed, forgiven, and called by name. Believe this good news, and live as God's people.

Benediction

In your baptism you have received the Holy Spirit, who reveals God's presence and love, and who empowers you to live as Christ's disciples. Go in peace to love and serve the Lord.

Transfiguration of the Lord

Helen Nablo

Exodus 34:29-35: After receiving the new tablets of the covenant, Moses comes down from the mountain, his face shining, to give to the people of Israel God's commandments.

Psalm 99: The psalmist sings the greatness of God, who spoke to the people in the pillar of cloud.

2 Corinthians 3:12–4:2: While Moses spoke to God with his face veiled, the Spirit of the Lord has removed the veil from our faces, granting us freedom and allowing us to see the glory of the Lord.

Luke 9:28-36 (37-43): Luke's story of the Transfiguration of Jesus.

REFLECTIONS

The Transfiguration of Jesus comes at a crucial time. When Peter confesses Jesus to be the Messiah (9:20), Jesus responds by offering up the first of his passion predictions: "The Son of Man must undergo great suffering, and be rejected by the elders, chief priests, and scribes, and be killed, and on the third day be raised" (9:21-22). Jesus says these things, but he has not yet made his way to Jerusalem where these things will come to pass. Whatever the Transfiguration is, it appears to be something that will prepare Jesus and Peter, James, and John for what is to come.

Many things are striking about the Transfiguration, and sermon possibilities abound. A part of the story I found particularly interesting is the description of what Moses, Elijah, and Jesus are talking about before the voice speaks, a detail Luke alone reports: They "were speaking of his departure, which he was about to accomplish at Jerusalem" (v. 31).

47

As an interim pastor, my work involves helping congregations deal with departures, with good-byes and letting go. I enter a church because a pastor has left; and soon, when the new pastor is found, the church will experience yet another good-bye. As I contemplated Luke's story of the Transfiguration, I began to search for a way to address not only Christ's departure in Jerusalem but also departures in a more general way. I was searching for a theme that would be helpful to Overbrook Church (the church I presently serve), a church that recently said good-bye to their much-loved pastor of seventeen years. My hope was to link this glorious text to a more common experience, that of preparing to face a good-bye, an ending—so that, in hearing, the congregation might feel more confident about their own capacity to experience God in the often difficult and challenging act of saying good-bye.

A SERMON BRIEF

When Our Faces Shine

Standing recently with a group of pastors, the topic of this week's lectionary text came up. "Oh, Transfiguration Sunday. . . . I *hate* Transfiguration Sunday!" one preacher said, while heads all around nodded in agreement. I must confess this text isn't my favorite to preach either! The problem, if I could put it in a nutshell, is "I never . . ." as in "I never have had an experience of God so dramatic, so awe-inspiring—and because I never have had such an experience, I really don't know what to do with Jesus up there on the mountaintop either."

But recently I heard a story of a woman who was overwhelmed by her life. Her grandchild, severely handicapped, required hours and hours of therapy; and she regularly helped out. But one day, working hard on "patterning," getting this child to make his hands and fingers do things in hopes that one day he would be able to pick up a fork or spoon by himself, this woman and her daughter-in-law came to verbal blows. It wasn't the first time this had happened, but this time it really hurt. It took three adults to get through a session, so this grandmother stayed on; but by the end of it she was in tears. At the end of her rope—feeling angry, hurt, defeated—she went home and took a bath. Sinking into the water, sobbing out her sadness and rage, she cried out to God that she just couldn't take it anymore. Suddenly, just then, she had an experience, a vision of God. She says she saw

God's face, which she could only describe as light that washed over her, light that bathed her whole being in peace.

Sometime later that day she went to her husband's office. "What happened to you?" he asked. She looked different. Her face was shining, in the way that Moses' and Jesus' faces shone. "What happened to you?" he said; and she told him, knowing that from now on things were going to be different—because she knew that God was near, surrounding her with light and love.

Not long ago I heard a good definition of love: "Love depends upon the capacity to reach beneath the surface of persons, to feel and touch the seed of life hidden there. And love becomes a power when it is capable of evoking that seed and drawing it from its hiding place."[1] Perhaps when that woman took to her bath, it was not unlike Jesus taking to the mountain: Each put themselves in a place where divine love could reach them, reaching beneath the surface of fear and doubt to touch and enliven the seed within.

Though I know the woman who had that experience, I still have to admit I have never had an experience so dramatic, so profound, as she had—or as Jesus had. Then again . . . maybe I have. As an interim pastor serving other churches before this one, I have found that the most profound time of my ministry is often the time when I am preparing to say good-bye. Maybe it's me, about what's going on for me as I prepare to leave and let go, but still, I seem to see people's faces in a different light. I can even say I have seen faces shine.

So many memories of saying good-bye come to me, when I give them permission, that is. I remember how, over coffee and bagels, a church member who "wanted to say good-bye" was shooting all these questions at me about what I think about their church's future, and where I'm going to go next. But after a time, her eyes softened; and she began telling me about her own faith, about some people in the church who have been Christ figures for her. Looking at her, speaking her faith this way, I see her face shine. In a last lunch with a dear older person in the church, I am offered wisdom from her many years and lovely words of affirmation and encouragement for this part of the journey we've shared—and as we go to hug each other good-bye, I look at her, and her face shines. At a service of healing, held just weeks before my final Sunday, people whom I will likely not touch or perhaps even see again come forward to have their heads anointed with oil. They speak their need for reconciliation and healing. I see both their great need and their great faith, and I do believe their faces shine.

It's as if in departing there is a gift: a gift of faces transformed by God's light, snapshots I will carry with me as I go on. I often find that in the last few months of a ministry there is this experience of having a deeper connection with folk, time being made more precious because we are living in this knowledge that it does not last forever. I don't know what it is about good-byes, about our coming up against the endings of certain relationships; but it surely can bring forth more real, more honest, more authentic interactions. There is something about getting ready to take a bend in the road, something about parting, that makes us more real, and at the same time, more alive in God. It's as if the veil that separates us has been lifted, as it used to be lifted at that particular moment in the wedding ceremony. People often speak of seeing a godly light in the faces of those they love who are dying. Somehow, in good-bye, barriers that were there fall away, and we can see each other more clearly. We can see each other face to face. We can live in appreciation of the mystery of the other.

All this makes me wonder: do we have to be in big existential moments to see the light of God shining in each other's faces? Might it not be possible to have this deeper connection, this awareness of God in one another's faces more often, more regularly?

I once heard Madeleine L'Engle say that the thing about Jesus is that he was never separated from the Source. Perhaps what blocks us from experiencing this deep and regular connection to the Source and also to and with each other is fear and this veil of self-protection we put up around ourselves, hoping to shield ourselves from endings that bring pain to our souls. We try to be the makers of our own destiny rather than open ourselves to God as the author of our destiny, as Jesus did. We try to avoid painful endings rather than trust God is with us as Alpha and Omega, beginning and end. But sometimes, the veil is lifted. Sometimes our defenses fall away, and we too are awash with light.

I have never had a mountaintop experience like Jesus had. Or maybe I have. Maybe you have too. Maybe one day, when a new pastor for this church is called and it is time for me to go, for us to say good-bye, we will have such an experience together—if we let God reach down below the surface of our lives, if we let God call forth the strength and courage and faithfulness that rests there within, ready to be enlivened. Maybe the transfiguration happens whenever God meets us in the place of our deepest need, breaking through our hardened exteriors and changing us.

So we can go on—go on living in this world of need with steadfast courage, gratitude for God's grace, and maybe even a shining face.

SUGGESTIONS FOR WORSHIP

Call to Worship

LEADER: Listen to the teaching of the Lord.
PEOPLE: **Let us turn our ears to God's words.**
LEADER: Let us remember the Lord's glorious deeds,
PEOPLE: **And rejoice in the wonders of God!**

Benediction

May God, Alpha and Omega,
abide with you all your journey long.
May Jesus, radiant in his glory,
be the light that lights your way.
And may the Holy Spirit, God's power alive in the world,
inspire, encourage, and renew you,
this day and forevermore. Amen.

1. From *The Symbolic and the Real: A New Psychological Approach to the Fuller Experience of Personal Existence* (New York: Julian, 1963).

Ash Wednesday

Sue A. Ebersberger

Joel 2:1-2, 12-17: The prophet calls for the people of Judah to make a deliberate decision to repent and return to God, proclaiming, "Rend your hearts and not your clothing."

Psalm 51:1-17: This is a classic psalm of penitence and the forgiveness of sins. "Create in me a clean heart, O God and put a new and right spirit within me."

2 Corinthians 5:20b–6:10: Paul speaks of God's unconditional love and the burdens one bears and the joys one has living a life of faith. We have ". . . the weapons of righteousness."

Matthew 6:1-6, 16-21: Jesus commands people to fast and pray because they are called to do so by God, not because they will gain recognition. Centering one's life on God is also central to the message.

REFLECTIONS

Ash Wednesday marks the beginning of the Lenten season. Lent traditionally has been a time of fasting and prayer, self-examination and study, and works of love. In today's world, these practices have been lost or greatly diminished at best. They are practices that help us shake free our souls from the many things that entangle them so that we may repent and turn toward God.

I was drawn in particular to the Joel passage that talks about "rending our hearts" and then making a deliberate action to turn around and move toward God. While the text speaks to a community facing difficult times now and in the future, the text also speaks to us individually when we are experiencing a crisis. "Rending our hearts" happens when things are thrust upon us from the outside as well as when our conscience nags at us on the inside. God's gracious love and patience is something we can rely on in these times.

A SERMON BRIEF

Rend Your Heart

Mark was a self-made man. He grew up in a small town in Texas, went to schools at the poor end of town, and struggled to make ends meet when he went to college. He got married just after graduation. Mark and his wife, Kathy, struggled during those early years of their marriage—wondering where the money would come from to pay the rent and buy food and all the things needed for their home.

Somewhere along the way things got a little easier financially. Mark got a job working in New York City. The commute from Philadelphia wasn't too bad; it was only an hour and a half each way on the train. He put in twelve-hour days so that his company would know that he was a hard worker. And then there were the business trips that took him away from home for a week or two at a time. He offered to have Kathy go with him to exciting places around the world—Paris, Moscow, the Riviera—but she didn't want to leave the babies at home. So he went by himself.

One night, twenty years later, Mark walked in the door after a two-week trip to be greeted by Kathy saying, "Welcome home, dear. By the way, I don't want to be married to you anymore." Mark stared at her in shock. He almost stopped breathing. Every ounce of business savvy leaked out of his body. For the first time in his life, Mark was speechless as his heart was ripped with each word she spoke.

"Rend your heart and not your clothes," said the prophet Joel. Sometimes things that happen to us tear our souls.

Sarah, a delightful thirty-year-old single woman, had a full life but desperately wanted to be married. At the law office, she found herself working closely with Allen, a charming but married man. Allen paid a lot of attention to Sarah. While she liked the attention, she ignored it as best she could because he wasn't available.

One evening the two of them were working late into the night, Allen began to pour out his heart to Sarah. He wasn't happy in his marriage. He wanted out. He wanted to spend the rest of his life with someone just like Sarah. Upon hearing this, Sarah's heart melted and the two of them started to see each other.

But feelings of guilt and remorse began nagging at Sarah's

conscience. Sarah watched her best friend's expression cloud up every time she mentioned Allen's name. Sarah couldn't even bring herself to tell her parents about Allen. What would they think about their only daughter seeing a married man? And people at the office had begun to whisper to each other after Allen would stop by her desk to say hello. She knew, deep in her heart, that this relationship was wrong. Sadness, pain, jealousy, and shame—all took their turns cutting away at Sarah's heart.

"Rend your hearts and not your clothes," says the prophet Joel. Sometimes things inside of us tear our hearts.

Rending our hearts makes us open to the transforming power of God's love. When our hearts are insulated with self-indulgence, when our hearts are encrusted with feelings of shame or doubt, fear or anger, God's light cannot shine through and make us whole.

As we enter Lent on this Ash Wednesday, we come with our own hurts and needs. We desperately want to be made whole. We come, knowing that we need to come in faith, to reach out to God and others, to touch each other's souls. And yet, we hold back.

Sometimes we are afraid to come in faith, because that one thing that we are asking for might not happen—and then we lose our faith! At times we come with our faith in our heads, asking questions that keep God as a concept. Our fears and our minds keep us separated from God. Rend your heart and sweep out your soul.

Sometimes, we need to reach rock bottom before we are able to turn around and reach for God's outstretched hand. Sometimes we need to spend all our mental and emotional energies before we are able to offer our broken hearts to God. We need to exhaust our souls before we are able to breathe in the breath of the Holy Spirit.

What's in your heart, mind, soul, or body that zaps your energy, imagination, and joy? What keeps you from offering your heart to God? God's healing brings about wholeness. Healing is not a cure. Healing is being made right with God and other people. Healing allows us to have a new perspective on what is happening in our lives.

Use this Lenten season to spend time reflecting on the places in your life that are broken and need to be healed, the places that are empty and need to be filled. Joel invites you to come rend your heart and offer it to God.

SUGGESTIONS FOR WORSHIP

Call to Confession

Friends, begin this holy season by admitting your need for repentance and forgiveness. Relying on God's promise of redemption, let us confess our sins together.

Prayer of Confession

Steadfast God, you called us forth and breathed life into us so that we could serve you. In the busyness of life, we forget that without your breath we are but bits of clay. It is easier to make public acts of confession than to live our lives as though we truly believed our confession. It is easier to say "This is too hard; I can't" than to rely on your power to get us through. We are afraid to look into the face of our own mortality, knowing that one day we will return to dust. Give us strength and courage to face all that comes our way in this life. Through Christ our Lord. Amen.

Assurance of Pardon

God created you and loves you and will always forgive you when you turn toward God honestly. Know that your sins are forgiven and be at peace.

The Imposition of Ashes

Say to each person: "Remember that you are dust and to dust you shall return. Through it all, know that you are God's beloved child."

First Sunday in Lent

Kitty Cooper Holtzclaw

Deuteronomy 26:1-11: The Lord commands the offering of first fruits and tithes as the Israelites settle into the land promised to their ancestors.

Psalm 91:1-2, 9-16: God is praised as the refuge and defender of those who love God.

Romans 10:8*b*-13: Those who confess Jesus Christ as Lord will be saved.

Luke 4:1-13: Jesus is tempted in the wilderness before he begins his ministry.

REFLECTIONS

A major theme of the Lenten season is the preparation for Easter by performing spiritual "spring cleaning" of our lives. As we received the ashes on our foreheads on Ash Wednesday, we heard one of two things: "Remember you are dust and to dust you will return," or "Repent and believe the gospel." Traditionally, this is a time to pay special attention to the things that separate us from being able to experience resurrection in our lives.

This sermon examines the temptations of Jesus and his response to them. In it, I have attempted to equip worshipers with the ability to recognize and stand firm against some of the temptations they face.

A SERMON BRIEF

As children, we have ambitious dreams. We want to be ballerinas, astronauts, professional athletes, and artists. We want to dance, to soar, and to create things that enrich our lives and the lives of others. But those childhood dreams soon give way to reality. Someone tells us we are good at art, so maybe we should be architects. Since we are athletic, we can play on the church softball team when we finish school. Since we like science, maybe we can be science teachers or nurses. And our childhood dreams are realized as just that—dreams— and are put to practical use in our daily jobs. We proudly pay for our own groceries for the first time and think we have arrived. We may have given up dancing or soaring or flying, but we are not long in the real world before we begin to realize that there must be something more than just getting up every day, paying bills, and fighting death and taxes. Life must be more than just surviving.

We soon find out that we must make some choices, make some concessions. We train our children early in this. We teach them to say no to television and yes to homework. (At least we try.) But even when both choices are equally good, saying yes to one thing automatically means saying no to some other things. If I say yes to reading, I am automatically saying no to folding clothes or cutting grass. Each and every day, we choose between thousands of yesses and noes.

In Romans, Paul is clear about the source of meaning and integrity for living. Our guide in decision making is the Lordship of Jesus Christ. He puts it in such a simple way that we ask, "What's the catch?" Actually, confessing Jesus is Lord is the most complex yet simple thing we can ever do, for it affects our whole lives. Paul joins the confession of the mouth with the belief of the heart. We might describe it as being and doing, that our actions match our values. When we say yes to the Lordship of Jesus Christ, we automatically say no to the lordship of anyone or anything else. The Luke passage shows us that the things we say no to are as definitive as the things to which we say yes.

Jesus walks up out of the waters of his baptism and is led straightway into the wilderness by the Holy Spirit. Then the devil shows up. The devil offers Jesus three good things: bread, power, and the opportunity to impress a large number of people so they will listen to him. These are good things. Jesus could feed himself—a good thing—and he could feed all the hungry people of the world—another good thing. Since he is Jesus, he certainly would use power appropriately and for good, so why not? Surely it would jumpstart his ministry if he did something spectacular. He could build disciples right away. He would have so many people knocking at his door that he could pick and choose from the brightest and best.

What the devil is doing in his offers, though, is challenging two different things: the identity and the methods of Jesus, his being and his doing. At his baptism, Jesus had heard the voice of God saying to him, "You are my Son, the Beloved; with you I am well pleased." The devil comes to him at his weakest moment and says, "*If* you are the Son of God, . . . come on now. *If* you have the stuff, show me." The devil is challenging him at his most basic levels—who he is as a human being and who he is as a divinity. All that Jesus had to do was change a rock into something like Mother just pulled out of the oven. Then his suffering would be over.

But God's way is not to demand devotion out of fear or manipulation but to offer love and receive love in return. So no matter how innocent turning a stone into bread may seem to us, Jesus says, "No." He does not say, "No, thank you for considering my needs." He does not say, "Not right now. Perhaps I will consider your offer at a later date." In a fashion that leaves no doubt where his motivation and loyalty lay, echoes resound throughout the canyon: "No, no, no . . ."

So the devil offers him some things he may find a little more interesting—power and glory. Notice that all these things the devil offers are really God's property already. They are things of which Jesus is worthy, but he says no to all of it. These noes are, in fact, the very first words recorded in his ministry. They tell us that Jesus is not totally inclusive. Jesus does not embrace any and every thing. Through his noes, we learn what is important to him and how he will live his life and die his death. He will not use the power and authority given to him by God for his own benefit. He will not change creation, including us, to meet his need for comfort or convenience. Rather he will meet us in creation as we are so he can meet our need for salvation.

Jesus used the little word no to respond to every one of the devil's challenges. He said no to the devil on the most basic issue of life and on the grandest issues of glory. And he said no to the devil on what came between, too, which is all the kingdoms of the world.

It is between these two extremes of survival and glory that Jesus spent most of his earthly days, and it is between these two that we spend most of ours. We spend our time in various physical and spiritual kingdoms called school, job, home, and church. These are of grand scope and range from the most basic human needs to the highest spiritual pinnacles. Like Jesus, we are tempted at all these levels. But because of the power of the Holy Spirit within us, we are given the strength to say no to temptation. The devil does not waste time tempting us with sin we cannot commit. We are only tempted with what is within our grasp.

I am not saying that saying no to the devil is an easy or even a simple thing to do. But I am saying that we have great power to resist evil because Jesus is on our side, fighting with us and for us, even to the death. One of my favorite hymns is "A Mighty Fortress Is Our God" by the Protestant reformer Martin Luther. In his hymn Luther warns us that "still our ancient foe doth seek to work us woe." Because of the foe's great "craft and power," as well as his "cruel hate," there is nothing on earth that can equal him. Even though our strength is not great enough, God has chosen "the right man" to be on our side, his Son Christ Jesus. This means that we do not need to fear, "though this world, with devils filled, should threaten to undo us." One of the verses says, "The Prince of Darkness grim, we tremble not for him; . . . one little word shall fell him." Jesus knew that one little word. Do you?

SUGGESTIONS FOR WORSHIP

Call to Worship (adapted from Psalm 91:1-2 and Romans 10:9, 12-13)

LEADER: You who live in the shelter of the Most High, will say to the Lord,

PEOPLE: **You are my refuge and my fortress; my God in whom I trust.**

LEADER: If you confess with your lips that Jesus Christ is Lord and believe in our heart that God raised him from the dead, you will be saved.

PEOPLE: **The same Lord is Lord of all and is generous to all who call on him.**

LEADER: Everyone who calls on the name of the Lord shall be saved.

PEOPLE: **Thanks be to God!**

Prayer of Confession

Generous God, you have given us a rich inheritance to possess. Forgive us for forgetting the source of our blessings. Forgive us for forgetting the ways you have been faithful to us throughout our years and before. Forgive us for relying on our feeble strength to remain faithful. Restore our thankfulness and our trust in you. Amen.

Assurance of Pardon

The word is near you, on your lips and in your heart. Accept the gift of your salvation, for in Jesus Christ, we are forgiven. Amen.

Benediction

Carry the Word of God in your heart and model it in your life. Rely on the Holy Spirit to strengthen and guide you in the ways of God. Celebrate the bounty that God has given you. Amen.

Second Sunday in Lent

Sandra Sonhyang Kim

Genesis 15:1-12, 17-18: Despite Abram's childlessness, God promises him that his descendants will be as numerous as the stars in the sky and seals that promise with a covenant.

Psalm 27: The psalmist confidently declares God's presence in the midst of trouble, for the Lord is "my light and my salvation."

Philippians 3:17–4:1: Paul encourages the believers in Philippi to "press on toward the goal" of God's call in Christ Jesus.

Luke 13:31-35: Jesus weeps over his beloved city of Jerusalem and desires to gather its "children together as a hen gathers her brood under her wings."

REFLECTIONS

After a long talk with my three-year-old daughter we have come to an agreement. We both made a "pinky promise" and sealed it with a thumb stamp. Less than a minute later she was engaged in the same behavior that caused us to have the previous long talk. Fixing my eyes on her, I complained, "But, but, we just made a promise!" To my dismay, as she was running up the stairs, she said, "I don't promise, I don't promise, Mommy!"

The story of oath making that the Genesis text relates is difficult for most modern readers to comprehend. Like my three-year-old girl, we not only take promises lightly, we also do not make serious oaths by cutting animals in half as our text describes. Subsequently when we encounter the Genesis story, it raises many questions in the reader's mind: What is the nature of the oath? Why were the birds not cut? What is the significance of the oath? However the most mind-boggling question it raises for many readers is the feasibility of God being bound by such an oath.

While we do not have satisfying answers to all the questions, there is one biblical analogy that throws some light onto this text. In Jeremiah 34, Judah is being condemned for her faithlessness. The prophet Jeremiah declares the fate of Judah will be the same as the slaughtered calf that was passed through by a community of people who participated in an act of oath making. In this kind of oath, when participants pass through divided animals, they are promising that should they be unfaithful to the terms of the oath they will be punished like the slaughtered animals. It is, indeed, a serious oath. Thus it is worth noting that in the Genesis text God not only makes this kind of oath with Abram but is the only participant in such an oath. It is beyond our comprehension to know the motivation behind God's action. However, if we remind ourselves of God's love shown in the incarnation of Jesus and his painful death on the cross, perhaps the God who walked between the slaughtered animals is not so foreign after all—even to twenty-first century Christians who often shout "I don't promise, I don't promise!" to nullify promises.

A SERMON BRIEF

The terrorist attack of September 11, 2001, has left us many tearful stories. I remember crying often after the attack. I cried on one crisp September morning when I heard the number of estimated victims; I cried when the names of the victims were called the next day; I cried one rainy afternoon when I saw their family members and friends who walked around the site of the attack in a desperate search with loved ones' pictures around their necks. But the one story that made me weep streams of tears was the story of the firefighters. With firm determination to search for any survivors, they went into the life-threatening pile of debris over and over again. For some of them, there they ended their lives, often in exchange for the pursuit of other lives. When I think about the firefighters, however, I remember one voice most vividly. It was a voice I heard on a National Public Radio station of a 72-year-old retired firefighter who came to volunteer not too long after the tragic incident. With a promise to come back the next day after caring for his aching back, he was asked why he had come to this dreadful site. He said,

"This is what I promised to do when I took an oath to become a fire-fighter."

This made a deep impression on me because I am the kind of person who checks the return policy before every purchase to make sure I am not forever bonded to what I buy. Promise making is not one of my favorite activities, because of the burden of prolonged promise keeping and the potential fear of promise breaking. Thus, oath making that reminds me of the seriousness of a court scene will be at the very bottom of my list of things to do. Perhaps this is why the voice of that heroic old man still rings in my ears from time to time and makes me wonder what is it about the promise that held this man to be faithful for such a long time and motivated him to come to rescue victims of the attack despite the grave danger he would face.

In Genesis 15, we encounter a promise that God makes with Abram. Abram rescued his nephew Lot and many others from the kings who had defeated Sodom and Gomorrah and brought back goods that had been stolen. "After these things," as the opening of our story says, God meets Abram and makes a covenant promising descendants and land to Abram. "O Lord God, how am I to know that I shall possess it?" Abram pleads to God. And God, in answer, instructs Abram to bring various animals and cut them in half and lay them opposite each other. When Abram had done what God had requested, God passed through the cut animals as a smoking fire pot and a flaming torch. "On that day the Lord made a covenant with Abram," we are told, a promise that God will indeed grant descendants as numerous as the stars in the heaven and a vast land for his forthcoming generations to inhabit.

Although the content of the promise made is not unfamiliar to Abram or to the readers, the way the covenant was made is unique. We notice that, unlike previous promises made to Abram, here God makes the oath by passing through the slaughtered animals. And if we think about the seriousness of this bloody scene we would detect that this is not an ordinary promise that we make when we sign a credit card bill at a local restaurant after dinner. Rather, this is an oath of self-imprecation, which is a serious way of reminding Abram: With my whole being I promise to uphold and protect this covenant I made onto myself before you. And should I break this oath, may my fate be as the slaughtered animals. Thus, it is not a big surprise that some commentators have had difficulty with God who is the sole participant in the oath making of this text. It is equally hard for many of us to conceive of God as being bonded by an oath or to fathom God having the same fate as the animals: crushed, cut, and dead.

Then again, strangely, these rather gruesome words—crushed, cut, and dead—are not unfamiliar for many Christians. Especially during the season of Lent, these images resonate in the minds of many Christians. We see a good deal of rather graphic pictures of a man who was crushed. We hear numerous melodies sung about a man who was cut. We frequently read passages narrating the story of a man who died having the same fate as the slaughtered animals. And with an identification of this man as the Son of God, perhaps we are allowed to witness a glimpse of God who exclusively participated in an oath of self-imprecation long ago.

The old firefighter I heard on the radio could not know what his oath would require of him; but when he made it, he promised to live by it.

God, fully knowing that it would require being crushed, cut, and slaughtered, not only made an oath to Abram but made a similar oath to humankind, and in doing so gave God's love to the world in the gift of Jesus Christ.

SUGGESTIONS FOR WORSHIP

HALF OF THE CONGREGATION: With love God made a promise to Abram by walking through the animals that were crushed, cut, and slaughtered.

THE OTHER HALF OF THE CONGREGATION: With love God made a promise to all of us through Jesus Christ who was crushed, cut, and slaughtered.

EVERYONE: Let us worship God, knowing that God invites all of us to celebrate that everlasting promise of love in Jesus Christ.

Prayer of Confession

You call us to receive the oath of your unfailing love through Jesus Christ who died for us; yet we go astray and go our own ways, abandoning your faithful love. Forgive us and restore us as we seek to live in your everlasting covenant of love today.

Assurance of Pardon

Through Jesus Christ God has made an everlasting covenant of love with us. By means of this love we are confident that we are forgiven and redeemed.

Benediction

As a community of God's everlasting covenant in Christ Jesus who gave himself for us, may we be faithful to God, knowing that the abundant love of this covenantal God goes with us this day, through this season of Lent, and forever more.

Third Sunday in Lent

Kerra Becker English

Isaiah 55:1-9: A reminder of God's covenantal promise to care for the nation of Israel, and an extension of that blessing to everyone who thirsts that they may come to the waters and receive God's grace without paying a price.

Psalm 63:1-8: The psalmist longs for connection with God, and likens that connection to being "satisfied as with a rich feast."

1 Corinthians 10:1-13: A warning not to fall into idolatry and immorality as the wanderers in the wilderness did—even though they were fed with the same spiritual food and drank the same spiritual drink from the rock that is Christ.

Luke 13:1-9: The parable of the fig tree warns that one must repent and bear fruit or else be cut down and perish just as Jesus' examples of those who refused to repent were struck with sudden calamity.

REFLECTIONS

Lent seems an unusual time to read such passages about rich feasts and unearned delights when the season more characteristically carries the tone of sacrifice. In recent years, Lent has become just another reason to start a diet instead of being a time to fast from the world's marks of success and to learn to live by God's gifts and graces. But in the liturgical practice, it helps to remember that the Sundays of Lent do not count. They are not a part of the forty days of the season. Sundays are to be the feast days, resurrection days, the liturgical reminder that God's blessings continue to be poured out even in the deserts and temptations of daily life. God does not let our hunger go unfed. God will not let our thirst dry us back to the dust. God's love is steadfast and sure, and God's people will *not* be forever forsaken.

These moments when the dawn breaks through the darkness are truly signs of God's blessing—where the wine and milk are bought without price in a culture that continues to remind us "we get what we pay for." This food metaphor in Isaiah is a perfect way of conveying how God, who is beyond our comprehension, can touch us even in our daily lives, through our daily bread. Food touches all of our senses: sight, smell, taste, feel, and—because food is the perfect excuse for getting together with other people—we even *hear* what Grandma used to tell us as she stood next to the stove mashing potatoes. Family covenants are written through our eating habits, and as Jesus' own brothers and sisters, the bread of life and the cup of salvation promise new hope as we share the meal we have inherited as welcome guests at Jesus' own family table.

A SERMON BRIEF

Food is life. Without food, we perish. We mark special occasions by eating together with family and friends. We are quick to talk about the pleasure of enjoying a well-prepared feast that tantalizes both the eye and the palate. Nothing is quicker to comfort, stronger to satisfy than a meal that evokes a heartfelt memory. None other than Jesus charged his disciples to remember him by eating and drinking so that they might share in his bodily experience of laying down his life for his friends. The bread becomes more than risen wheat; it becomes the risen life. The wine becomes more than aged grapes; it becomes an age-old covenant of forgiveness.

But during Lent, many deprive themselves of the gastronomical delights. In observance of the sacrifices Jesus made on our behalf, we use this penitential time to start a new diet, give up chocolate or other sweets, or perhaps take a fast from our alcohol consumption. What used to be the ritual observance of "fish Fridays" for Roman Catholics has become culturally adapted to accommodate a much more subtle awareness of our own gluttony. The Lenten fast reminds us that everything we have comes from God, but it also reminds us that everything we take or hoard contributes to the poverty level that allows starvation still to happen all around the world.

So why is it that we come to this scripture reading talking about buying wine and milk without price, delighting in rich food, and being satisfied as with a rich feast? Is that just to tempt us to greater and more savory sins? Or is it to remind us of something deeper, something more intrinsic to the good news of the gospel?

I think it's the latter. There is incredibly good news in this text about God's economy that promises enough for everyone and God's willingness to abundantly pardon our sins and shortcomings. Everyone, *everyone* who thirsts, Isaiah tells us, is welcome to come to the waters. Those who have no money are bidden to come and buy wine and milk without price. In a dry and weary land, God's steadfast love seems better than life, and our souls are satisfied in God's goodness as with a rich feast. In recent years, the Lenten observance for me has become less about "giving up" and more about "giving over" to God's ways of providing. For God's ways are higher than our ways and God's thoughts higher than our thoughts. God's grace abounds even in the dryness, even in the barrenness, even in the times we are without money, or are spending our money and labor for that which does not satisfy. God breaks through our hunger and thirst and fills us with good things.

I heard a story some time ago that has penetrated my heart and reminded me yet again of how God breaks through our darkest moments to bear witness to the light that is life. A friend of a friend was pregnant with her second child. At about the fifth or sixth month, well into the pregnancy, the worst that could happen happened. This young woman and her husband were told by their physician that the baby was dead. The funeral for this baby nearly buried their hope. They were devastated, dry, and spiritually broke. After some weeks, they needed something to pull them out of their sullen spirits, so they made reservations at their favorite Italian restaurant. It was a night to remember—and to forget. They ordered appetizers, expensive entrees, more than one bottle of wine, and finished their grand meal with desserts and cappuccino. They didn't worry about the cost. It was much more important to laugh again, to hope again, to be a couple again.

But when the bill came, they received the biggest surprise of all; their bill had been paid in advance. What they didn't know was that the husband's boss had lost a child too, an infant who died from SIDS. He knew their pain, and met them in that pain. Shortly after discovering what had happened, he called their favorite restaurant. He told the restaurant owner, "No matter what they order, whenever they come in next, I want to pay the check." The restaurant owner was quick to honor this request, for he too shared a similar grief and was delighted to bring this message of joy. The year before, his college-age son had been killed in an automobile accident. Mere coincidence? I don't think so.

God is the one orchestrating such events. For it is God who meets us in our deepest pain, and says, "Come, buy wine and milk without money and without price. Listen carefully to me, and eat what is good, and delight yourselves in rich food. Incline your ear, and come to me; listen so that you may live."

I have been to the very same Italian restaurant. They serve extraordinary meals, but this particular meal truly embodied God's love served to satisfy a hunger deeper than can be met even by the homemade manicotti and rum cake for dessert. This meal was communion: a common union these families shared in the deepest grief that can only be penetrated by the beneficent and magnificent love of God.

Our observance of Communion, our celebration of the Lord's Day is met with the same pain and joy intermingled with one another. Jesus died so that we might live, and live not just from heartache to heartache, but live by knowing God's true abundance. God's word of joy goes out to all people, and it doesn't come back empty. God's word accomplishes its purposes and succeeds in its mission. Sometimes it takes our hands and our hearts to fulfill the intent, but the briars and thorns of life dare not have the final word. The final culmination of the Lenten season is not the hopelessness of Good Friday, but the ecstasy of Easter morning. Christ is risen! Christ is risen indeed!

SUGGESTIONS FOR WORSHIP

Call to Confession

The grace of God has dawned upon the world, offering healing for all humankind. No matter who we are, or what we've done, or what we haven't done, God's grace is sufficient for us all.

Prayer of Confession (based on Isaiah 55)

O God, your economy judges all worthy to receive milk, and wine, and bread without cost. Our economy has made the rich richer and the poor poorer. We are quick to spend our money for that which is not bread and to labor for that which does not truly satisfy. We greedily accept the rich feast for ourselves when the rest of the world suffers near starvation. Help us to right our wrongs, and forgive us when we don't know where to begin. In your mercy, keep your covenant of abundance with all peoples and speak boldly to us that we may hear of your grace and live. Amen.

Words of Assurance (based on Psalm 63)

In a dry and weary land where there is no water God's love will quench your thirst. God's steadfast love is better for us than life. Know that you are forgiven. Know that your deepest hungers will be satisfied. Know that God watches over you in the darkest night, and be at peace.

Fourth Sunday in Lent

Ruthanna B. Hooke

Joshua 5:9-12: The first Passover is celebrated in the land of Canaan. The gift of manna ceases as the people depend on provisions of their new land.

Psalm 32: The Lord forgives the transgressions of those who acknowledge their sin and restores believers to a place of joy and safety.

2 Corinthians 5:16-21: Anyone who is in Christ is a new creation.

Luke 15:1-3, 11b-32: In response to condemnation from the scribes and Pharisees, Jesus teaches in parables, including the parable of the lost son.

REFLECTIONS

The theme of "home" captures my attention in the story of the prodigal son. This parable is beloved and powerful partly because it draws on universal human experiences—being far from home, being homeless, coming home—in order to illuminate our relationship with God. In the parable, the younger son's experience of being far from home is a metaphor for human estrangement from God. Conversely, being "at home" means to be in right relationship with God. It is a state of being rather than a place, hence the elder son feels exiled although he has not physically left home.

As in the parable, in this sermon I draw on the experience of homelessness and homecoming to gain insight into our relationship with God. In doing so, I make an assumption suggested by the parable—namely that the human feeling of homesickness is at a deeper level a desire for God. This means that homesickness and homecoming are not just good metaphors for describing our relationship with God; but in fact these feelings themselves, experienced in our lives, point us toward God and will only be satisfied in God. The sermon presents our lives as a constant turning and returning toward the home we have in God's loving, forgiving presence. The sermon also accents the role of the father in the parable, who represents God's passionate longing for us to come home. The father is the central figure in this parable, reminding us that, in our lifelong journey home to God, God is the central character: It is God who seeks us out and brings us home, offering us more than we deserve or desire. The call of Lent and of life to return to God is an invitation proffered by God's love, to which we respond only through God's grace.

A SERMON BRIEF

The Journey Home

From time to time I see the signs, around my neighborhood: "LOST DOG: 2 year-old mutt. Answers to name: Zoe. We love her and miss her. REWARD." These signs bring two images into my head: One is of the dog, Zoe, running around the neighborhood, afraid, in danger, looking in vain for her home. The other picture is of her humans, searching the streets, calling her name, looking under porches and in sheds and garages. These signs and images are heart-rending. But it's not just that I feel for Zoe and her humans. I feel for all of us. For something about this predicament, the lost soul and the people frantically seeking her, is very familiar.

We love the story of the prodigal son so much because we *know* this story. There is something about the predicament of *both* sons in this story that is so familiar to us. We have all felt as exiled and lost as they did, far from God, our home, our true selves.

The story tells us of two ways this can happen. The younger son took the path of self-destruction. He deliberately turned his back on his family and his home and left. Then he spent everything he had. Eventually, when he was starving, he found himself taking care of pigs for a Gentile—the ultimate shame for a Jew. He wound up as far from himself and his God as he could be. But the worst thing for him to contemplate, as he sat alone, hungry, not even knowing who he was anymore, is that he *chose* all of this. He did not have to leave his home, but he did.

The older son loses himself not by being self-destructive, but by trying to be perfect. He never disobeyed any commands; he has worked diligently for his father for years. Yet he feels like a slave. He is exiled without even leaving home. Worst of all, like his brother, he chose to live this way. His father was there all along, but he refused to receive anything from him.

There are many ways that we can bring ourselves to the place of exile that these two brothers reach. We fall into self-destructive patterns where we fail to care for ourselves. We compromise our values until we no longer know what we stand for. We try to be perfect, never realizing that we are okay just as we are. The worst thing about these patterns is that on some level we *choose* to live this way. We are responsible for the ways we destroy the selves that God has given us.

Yet this story is not only about being exiled from God and ourselves; it is really about the journey home. It begins when the younger son is at his lowest point; and, inexplicably, he "comes to himself." He returns to the self that he lost and almost destroyed. He hears God's voice inside him saying, "Come home." Even more precious than this voice is what the younger son finds when he gets home. He assumes he will return to punishment. What meets him there is beyond what he could have imagined or deserved. The two sons' predicaments are familiar to us; but the father's behavior is *unfamiliar*, shocking, outrageous. Wouldn't it be fair for him to punish the son, make him prove that he had reformed? But that's not what happens. Instead, the father is so eager to welcome the son back that he makes a fool of himself. He *runs* to meet his son; he showers on him signs of favor; he uses up the best that he has. He is equally extravagant toward his older son. He leaves his own party to go find him and beg him to come in. He says to him, "*Everything* I have is yours." This father is as prodigal as his younger son is, but prodigal not in spending himself but in spending his love. He is a fool for love.

We love this story not because of the grim picture it paints of human sin, but because of the beautiful picture of God's love that it gives us. God comes out into the dark streets and looks under porches and anywhere God can think of to find us. God calls our name, deep inside of us, and begs us to come home. When we make the first gesture of returning, God runs out to us and showers us with more love than we can imagine or deserve. God makes a fool of God's self to get us back, and God will put up any reward for us, even to the point of giving God's life for us. To come home is to return to this reality, that we are God's Beloved. We don't have to be perfect, and we don't have to destroy ourselves. We can come home.

Sometimes it's hard to find our way to that home we have with God. That's why God puts up signs everywhere, saying, "I am looking for you. Come home." Zoe's humans put up signs that Zoe herself could not read, but I had a friend who put up a sign that her dog could read. She had lost her dog on a mountain. After she had spent hours searching, a friend suggested she put out an old shirt belonging to her. She laid the shirt out by the trailhead. The next morning she returned and sure enough, there was her dog curled up on the shirt.

God is so eager to find us and bring us home that God puts up signs, signs we can read, that tell us of God's presence and love. God lays out the shirt, so that we know where to find God. The church is full of such signs: Scripture is a sign; this community is a sign. The feast we will soon share is a sign. As you receive this precious food, see if you can hear in it God saying, "I have been looking for you everywhere. I love you and I miss you. Come home."

SUGGESTIONS FOR WORSHIP

Call to Worship

LEADER: O God, you have brought us to this life and this day.

ALL: **You have brought us to this place and to each other.**

LEADER: You have sought us out and found us.

ALL: **You have run to us and welcomed us home.**

LEADER: Open our hearts as we worship you this day.

ALL: **Help us to find you as you seek us, that we might be your people in the world.**

Prayer of Confession and Assurance of Pardon

LEADER: Let us confess our sins against God, our neighbor, and ourselves.

ALL: **Merciful God, we confess that we have wandered far from you, our home. We have not nurtured your image within us. We have not honored your image in our neighbor. We repent of these our sins. Speak to our listening ears. Bring us back from the distant country. Restore us to ourselves, to each other, and to you.**

LEADER: My friends, if any are in Christ, they are new cre-
            ations; the old has passed away; behold, the new has
            come. Your sins are forgiven. Your wholeness is
            restored. God welcomes you home. Amen.

Benediction

May the Spirit's voice be your guide.
May Christ's reconciliation be your mission.
May God's love be your home. Amen.

Fifth Sunday in Lent

Judith FaGalde Bennett

Isaiah 43:16-21: Through the prophet, God promises "to do a new thing."

Psalm 126: The people praise God for the great things God has done.

Philippians 3:4b-14: The accomplishments of Paul's earlier life are meaningless in light of his knowledge of Jesus Christ.

John 12:1-8: While visiting his friends in Bethany, Mary anoints Jesus' feet with costly perfume, prompting Judas's rebuke but Jesus' approbation.

REFLECTIONS

One of the joys of my life in recent years has been participating in an ecumenical discussion group formed originally by a group of progressive Catholics with an activist bent. These friends push me in two ways. First, they have led me to read a number of books I might not otherwise have chosen. Second, they force me to examine the state of my soul—and my lifestyle—on a regular basis.

Along the way, I have come to a new understanding of the radical nature of the gospel—and quite honestly I find it terrifying! Somehow, through the years, I had managed to avoid *really* looking at what faithfulness requires, and where Christ's sacrifice fits into the picture (not that I have ever been very comfortable with traditional explanations of the atonement). Moreover, I had fancied myself as something of a pacifist, until September 11, 2001. Since then, what is required of those who wish to follow the path of love in the face of violence has taken on another level of meaning altogether for me.

In approaching the story of Mary anointing Jesus' feet, in the con-

76

text of the raising of Lazarus and Jesus' own coming death, I find both a new poignancy and a new terror in the story of his inexorable journey toward Jerusalem. I find myself face-to-face with a different Jesus—not the Jesus who "died for our sins" but the Jesus who challenges us to lay down our own lives, if that is what is required to stop the world's journey toward self-destruction. The radical Jesus who asks us to be radical along with him is, in my experience, not the Jesus people in our pews want to hear much about; and I struggle with that. *How do we preach this Jesus?* Carefully, I suspect. This sermon is one small effort in that direction.

A SERMON BRIEF

Where We're Not Supposed to Be

My friend Pat and I were a part of what has come to be called "the first wave," that first large group of women who were ordained in this country beginning in the mid-seventies. Pat was the first woman to be appointed a supervising pastor or district superintendent in our annual conference, and the first to serve as dean of the cabinet. In that capacity, she was selected to preach the sermon for the opening worship service at the annual session, a highly symbolic moment for her clergy sisters. To mark the occasion, she vowed to wear her new red shoes! Our inside joke was that, if the going got rough, she could simply click her heels together and, like Dorothy in those storied "ruby red slippers," take herself back home to Kansas.

It was a marvelous sight, watching my church's leaders (such as the bishop, superintendents, and other annual conference dignitaries) process through the crowd and onto the platform at the front of the auditorium. There they all were, vested in white albs and red stoles (it was, after all, Pentecost), one pair of black oxfords after another, marching smartly along to the rhythms of the opening hymn—until, suddenly, a pair of bright red shoes! It was a moment of jubilation for Pat and all of us. So often in those days we experienced the discomfort of knowing that, in the eyes of many, we had invaded male space. Now, one of us had invaded that space and claimed it for us all.

In John's Gospel, Mary also invades male space, along with her sister Martha, at the dinner in the home of their brother, Lazarus. In the Mediterranean world in Jesus' time, men and women did not eat in the same place at the same time. Martha served the meal, which was acceptable behavior for a widow, which she could have been, but "her sister Mary's behavior was very inappropriate even for a widow."[1] Mary brought with her a pound of pure nard, a perfumed ointment imported from the Himalayas in alabaster boxes. In such a quantity, it would have been very costly. To have anointed Jesus' feet at all would have been unexpected; to have wiped his feet with her hair was a poignant gesture of tenderness, even intimacy.

Judas rebukes this woman who has invaded male space to perform an act of extravagance, but Jesus affirms both her presence and her gesture. In his eyes Mary is exactly where she should be. He has made it clear from the beginning of his public ministry that women, children, and other powerless folk of that day were welcome in his company. The coming reign of God would be a time and place where all were welcome, all were valued. Mary, in fact, demonstrated that new way of being together, in community, in mutuality.

This woman who goes where she is not supposed to go is important for another reason. Her brother Lazarus was dead, and now he is alive. This dinner is to celebrate that barrier-shattering event. He was dead, and the stench coming from his tomb was testimony to that reality. But Jesus was the life-bringer, the voice that called Lazarus forth from the stench; and now she would perfume his feet and fill their home with the sweet smell of life. Mary knew what the others were to learn in coming days. Jesus the life-bringer was himself under sentence of death, but his death would shatter that barrier once and for all, and Mary "got it"—in him was life.

But beyond these things, Jesus' affirmation of her presence and her understanding of who he was, there is more. Mary modeled the discipleship that will be required of all those who would follow Jesus. Soon he will press inexorably toward Jerusalem and that last meal together with his friends, where he will take off his robe and kneel like a servant to wash their feet. What Mary has done unbidden for him, he will do for his friends, drawing them "into intimate relationship with himself—the same intimate relationship that he enjoys with God."[2] Peter will protest, but Jesus will insist. The intimacy of foot washing removes the distance between Jesus and his followers, even as he demeans himself in the act, foreshadowing the humiliation of his coming death. As it draws them into closer relationship with him, it also "removes their alienation and estrangement from God."[3]

One more time, God is doing a new thing here. The extravagant act of a woman who went where she wasn't supposed to be becomes the explicit teaching of Jesus in his final hours. In a radical call to servanthood, he instructs his followers to do for each other what he has done for them. The reign of God to which he calls them—and us—requires the undoing of the world as we know it, with "all the ways in which humans are locked into each other and lock each other in."[4] In the process, we are likely to find ourselves in places we are not supposed to be, saying things we are not supposed to say, doing things we are not supposed to do.

But that is what the journey of Lent is all about; it is a journey of hard decisions, a time when we are reminded of the cost of following Jesus. Remember Mary as we move toward Palm Sunday and the events of Holy Week. She will be there with us, reminding us that life can come out of death, and that God is always ready to do a new thing, even in us.

SUGGESTIONS FOR WORSHIP

Call to Worship (adapted from Isaiah 43:16-21)

LEADER: Come, let us worship God who is doing a new thing:
PEOPLE: Now it springs forth, do you not perceive it?
LEADER: God will make a way in the wilderness and rivers in the desert.
PEOPLE: Our God gives water in the wilderness, drink to those who thirst.
LEADER: God has given us the breath of life,
PEOPLE: That we may declare our praise.

Prayer of Confession

God of new life, it is so much easier to follow the crowd and to do what is expected of us. We confess to you that we have heard you calling us from time to time, asking us to go where we're not sure we want to go, where we may not even be welcome. We ask your forgiveness for the times we have not listened, the times we have not obeyed. Walk close to us, O God, as we move through the wildernesses and deserts of our lives, that we may hear your voice clearly and heed it joyfully. This we ask in Jesus' name. Amen.

Assurance of Pardon (adapted from Psalm 126:1-6)

Even as God restored the fortunes of Zion, so God will do great things for us, if we but humbly ask. Those who sow in tears reap with shouts of joy. Our God welcomes us and offers forgiveness of all our sins.

Benediction (adapted from Philippians 3:4*b*-14)

Beloved, Christ Jesus has made us his own. If we would be like him, we must share in his suffering. Go now to continue your Lenten journey, forgetting what lies behind and straining forward to what lies ahead, knowing that it is the risen Christ who journeys with us. Go in his peace. Amen.

1. John J. Pilch, *The Cultural Dictionary of the Bible* (Minneapolis: The Collegeville Press, 1999), 68.
2. Frances Taylor Gench, *Women and the Word: Studies in the Gospel of John* (Louisville: Presbyterian Women, Presbyterian Church [USA], 2000), 43.
3. Ibid.
4. James Alison, *The Joy of Being Wrong: Original Sin Through Easter Eyes* (New York: Crossroad Publishing Company, 1998), 166.

Palm/Passion Sunday

Nancy Ellett Allison

Liturgy of the Passion

Isaiah 50:4-9a: The servant withstands humiliation with the strength of God.

Psalm 31:9-16: The psalmist pleads for God's deliverance amidst scorn and persecution.

Philippians 2:5-11: Christ's humility before his exaltation is to be the example for our faith.

Luke 22:14–23:56: Luke's telling of the passion and death of Jesus.

REFLECTIONS

The waving of palm branches holds great appeal for congregations. But perhaps this is the year to point out that Luke mentions no palms in his narrative. Perhaps this is also the year, the season, to prepare the congregation for what will surely lie ahead in their lives: suffering, pain, loss. When tragedy strikes, the question often brought to church is "Why?" Thoughtful minds will struggle for thoughtful answers in the midst of grief and in times of clear-headed reasoning. Yet asking "why" seldom brings satisfaction. It can never be answered well in the moment of crisis.

Bringing the question of "how" to suffering points all faces and hearts in another direction. Isaiah asserts that listening and yielding, clinging to God, will bring vindication. The psalmist lifts up a lament filled with grief and confidence in God's steadfast love. In Philippians we are pointed toward a kenotic life of humility and obedience as a way to imitate Christ. In Luke's passion narratives, Jesus models for us the way to prepare for the day of suffering that surely lies ahead.

A SERMON BRIEF

In the Day of Suffering

"I have eagerly desired to eat this Passover with you before I suffer . . ." (Luke 22:15).

Few of us know when suffering will envelope our lives. Yet in the last week of his life, Jesus marched with such resolve toward conflict with the religious power structure that he knew a passionate confrontation was inevitable. He knew it would be a time when his commitments to yielding, surrender, and identification with the oppressed would be severely challenged. In order to face this ordeal he prepared himself and his disciples for the struggle by establishing an emotional environment of intimacy and ritual. In transforming the Passover meal into a feast of remembrance, he established a practice that endures to this day. By retreating to a familiar place of prayer, he prepared himself spiritually and urged the disciples toward strength as well.

As a chaplain in an academic environment I once defined suffering, in the words of Eric J. Cassell, as "the distress brought about by the actual or perceived impending threat to the integrity or continued existence of the whole person."[1] Yet in that same medical center were living documents who defined their suffering in tears, whose pain was written on creased faces, whose continued, whole existence was already spent. Scholars also describe how "suffering is intensified by feelings of absurdity and eased by a sense of purpose."[2]

Elizabeth knew the absurdity. Three weeks she lay in a hospital bed to lengthen the gestation of her infant's inward days. Still the girl-child came too soon. So critically ill, neither parent could cuddle or cocoon her; she died, unheld by those whose love she owned. Elizabeth's existence was overwhelmed. She lashed out violently at her husband, cracking his shin with her heel. Her tongue-lashing severed the arteries, the nerves of the nurses who served her. The threat so took away her integrity, her very breath, that hyperventilating, Elizabeth collapsed at my feet. Stretched out on a table, when she would stir, we spoke to her in snatches. "You're safe now. Your husband loves you. God is with you. Remember your boys. You're safe now. . . ." Medications served the institution's purpose: to send her suffering to a different address.

Jesus chose a different path. He imbued his suffering with meaning and purpose, he said no to a violent response, and he engaged his friends with him in the trauma.

From the outset of his ministry Jesus spoke of God's compassion and urged repentance, a change of life. Miguel D'Escoto of Nicaragua saw this clearly. "We are not carrying the cross when we are poor or sick, or suffering small everyday things," he said. "They are all part of life. The cross comes when we try to change things. That is how it came for Jesus."[3] Jesus knew that his life lived in service to the least and the lowest would cost him all, and it was an intentional investment filled with purpose. For many of us, a contemplative life or the energy for radical and prophetic living begins in pain: when a search for new meaning, new identity is extracted from suffering.

In *Gravity and Grace,* Simone Weil asserts, "The false God changes suffering into violence. The true God changes violence into suffering."[4] It was the strength of his identity, integrity, and faith in God that allowed Jesus to experience abuse without retreating as a victim or responding in violence. When Judas approached Jesus in betrayal, he was questioned but not belittled. When the disciples, in their wild effort to protect Jesus, struck off the ear of a slave, the wounded man was touched with healing. When he was raised on a cross, Jesus called down God's forgiveness. Pain, frustration, fear can all lead to violence, but Jesus redirects our brutal emotions and responses toward the true God who suffers with us.

Often we, as much as Jesus, need to have a community around us to "experience" God's presence. When Jesus arranges for a furnished guest room in which to share the Passover meal with his disciples, he is creating a space where all can experience communion. He is gifting himself and the disciples with sustaining memories of time well spent. When Jesus implores the disciples to pray with him, it is a way of connecting them to his pain and grief. Even when he knows of Peter's betrayal, Jesus' eyes offer the cringing man his presence and forgiveness.

When suffering overwhelms, it can be better borne in community than in isolation. Sharing grief and pain, searching for meaning, encouraging clarity and honesty, struggling for faithfulness to long-voiced values, all create a fellowship that is more resilient than the individual acting alone. (Think of Tolkien's *The Fellowship of the Ring*.) When we, as a family of faith, strengthen our spiritual lives and our mutual communion through these practices, we too prepare ourselves for the day of suffering that will inevitably descend.

SUGGESTIONS FOR WORSHIP

Call to Worship

(based on the words of Jesus from the Passion Narrative)

ONE: The world says: "Take all you can. Use your body for gain."

MANY: **Jesus says: "This is my body, which is given for you."**

ONE: The world says: "An eye for an eye, a tooth for a tooth. Justice is required."

MANY: **Jesus says: "This cup that is poured out for you is the new covenant in my blood."**

ONE: The world says: "To be great is to be powerful. To be powerful is to have wealth. To have wealth is to be served."

MANY: **Jesus says: "The greatest among you must become like the youngest, and the leader like the one who serves."**

ONE: The world says: "In work and strength your worth will be known."

MANY: **Jesus says: "Pray that you may not come into the time of trial."**

ONE: The world says: "Might makes right. War is the only way to peace."

MANY: **Jesus says: "No more of this!"**

ONE: The world says: "The powers of evil control the fate of humanity."

MANY: **Jesus says: "From now on the Son of Man will be seated at the right hand of the power of God."**

ONE: The world says: "Racism is right. Sexism is fair. The poor are lazy. The earth is ours to abuse."

MANY: **Jesus says: "Father, forgive them; for they do not know what they are doing."**

ONE: The world says: "Live for today. Get what you can. There is no hope for tomorrow."

MANY: **Jesus says: "Truly I tell you, today you will be with me in paradise."**

ONE: The world says: "Protect yourself. Guard your emotions."

MANY: Jesus says: "Father, into your hands I commend my spirit."

ALL: Together we say: "Let us worship God in Spirit and in truth!"

Prayer of Confession and Assurance of Pardon (based on Isaiah 50:4-9*a*)

ONE: Come, let us confess in the presence of our Friend who seeks to strengthen us through prayer.

ALL: **God of grace and mercy, rather than sustaining the weary with words of hope, we burden them with idle chatter. When you seek to speak to us, we stop our ears with pounding music, ringing phones, and endless cable connections. When you call us to yield, we rebel in defiance. Teach us your ways that we might not be disgraced. Help us know your intimate presence and to trust your guiding hand. Amen.**

ONE: It is the Sovereign God who forgives us. Therefore none can declare us guilty. Through Christ we are empowered for new life. Amen.

Benediction

Fellow sufferers, go now in the strength of God, transformed by the grace of Christ, to live and serve in the fullness of the Spirit.

1. Eric J. Cassell, "Recognizing Suffering," *Hastings Center Report* 21, no. 3 (May-June 1991): 24.
2. C. Robert Mesle, *John Hick's Theodicy: A Process Humanist Critique, with a Response by John Hick* (Bedford: St. Martin's Publishing, 1991), 4.
3. Peter B. Price, "Living the Word: September 14," *Sojourners* 26, no. 5 (September-October 1997): 45.
4. Simone Weil, *Gravity and Grace* (New York: G. P. Putnam's Sons, 1952), 122.

Holy Thursday

Marsha M. Wilfong

Exodus 12:1-4 (5-10), 11-14: God gives Moses and Aaron instructions for the first Passover.

Psalm 116:1-2, 12-19: The psalmist offers thanks to God in response to deliverance from death.

1 Corinthians 11:23-26: Paul reminds the Corinthians of Jesus' words at the last supper with his disciples.

John 3:1-17, 31b-35: Jesus washes his disciples' feet and gives them a new commandment to love one another.

REFLECTIONS

In the epistle text, Paul reminds the Corinthians of Jesus' mandate for the institution of the sacrament of the Lord's Supper. In verse 26, Paul adds a brief commentary: "For as often as you eat this bread and drink this cup, you proclaim the Lord's death until he comes."

This sermon focuses on Jesus' instruction: "Do this in remembrance of me" (vv. 24 and 25). It addresses the question: What does it mean to "remember" Jesus through our celebration of the Lord's Supper? In that respect, it is more of a doctrinal sermon on the sacrament than an explication of the epistle lection per se. It draws generally on the Gospel narratives of Jesus' life, death, and resurrection and points to the significance of those events for our Christian life and faith.

At the same time, the sermon invites hearers to participate in the sacrament in an active, and perhaps a new, way—through theological remembering that makes a difference in the present. In terms of the celebration of the sacrament, it assumes that the congregation remains seated in the pews and the elements are passed from person to person.

A SERMON BRIEF

The words of institution of the Lord's Supper say, "Do this in remembrance of me." Jesus commanded his disciples, and he commands us, to remember him. But what kind of remembering are we to do when we celebrate the Lord's Supper? Are we to recall as many facts about Jesus' life, death, and resurrection as we can? Are we to reminisce about what a good, kind, loving person Jesus was? Are we simply to keep in mind that once upon a time—a significant time to be sure—Jesus did live, did die, and was resurrected from the dead? Our remembrance of him does include those things. But more than that, it is remembering that makes a difference now.

We do remember certain historical events. The words of institution point us to the last supper Jesus had with his disciples. Especially as we celebrate the Lord's Supper on this Holy Thursday, we remember *that* supper and the events that followed—Jesus' arrest, his trial before Pontius Pilate and Herod, his agonizing death on the cross. We remember that Judas betrayed him, that Peter denied him, that most of his followers deserted him at the hour of his death. We remember that he was buried in a tomb belonging to Joseph of Arimathea and that the women who went to the tomb on the third day after his death found it empty and were told, "He is not here. He is risen."

We remember also Jesus' life. His concern for the poor, the sick, the outcast. His love for children, and his love for those who turned away from him like the "rich young ruler," for those who deserted him like the disciples at his death, and even for those who sought to kill him. We remember his command to love one another, even as he has loved us—and his command to "Follow me," even to death on the cross.

And at this point perhaps, we remember ourselves. We remember that we don't always love one another—that selfishness or anger, hatred or indifference are as often the dominant characteristics of our relationships as is love. We remember that while we may *long* to follow Christ, we don't always *want* to—particularly if following Christ means sacrifice, risk, and denial of self. Like the "rich young ruler," we are apt to turn away when the word comes to "sell all you have and give to the poor," for we too have many possessions. Like Peter and the other disciples, we are apt to run when the going gets rough, not willing to risk our own necks. And like Judas, we are apt to betray him, when the way of Christ—the way of our faith—no longer seems to make sense in our world.

Yes, we do remember the historical events of Jesus' life, death, and resurrection—and are reminded in the process that we are sinners. And we can't help but note the contrast.

But our remembering does not stop there. We remember not only the events, but also the significance of those events. The death of Jesus was not just another death. We remember not just that a good man died a tragic death. We remember that *this* man died for us. We remember that, as in his life he took on our full humanity, so in his death he took on the burden of our sinfulness. The revelation that comes with his resurrection is that with his broken body our brokenness also died—our broken lives, broken promises, broken relationships with each other and with God. Through Christ's death and resurrection we have been given victory over all that seeks to break us, and have received forgiveness for all that we have broken. In our celebration of the Lord's Supper, we remember our brokenness and are freed for new life in Christ, for new life in community.

Our new life in Christ means new life as his body and communion with one another as members of his body. The very way in which we celebrate the Lord's Supper calls us to remember that. Though literally at a distance, symbolically we all sit together around the Lord's Table. We serve one another the bread and the cup. We act as Christ toward one another and are called to see Christ in each other. As we serve each other tonight, we may or may not be aware of the brokenness of the people around us. But our remembering of Christ calls us to be ministers of healing to one another—not just now in the serving of these elements, but tomorrow, and next week, in the everydayness of our lives.

"Do this in remembrance of me." Our celebration of the Lord's Supper makes a difference, not just because we eat this bread and drink from this cup. No, the difference it makes has to do as well with the kind of remembering we do—remembering that includes response: a response of confession of our own brokenness, a response of acceptance of the wholeness that God offers us, a response of acting on that wholeness in our relationships with God, with each other, with ourselves. That sounds like a tall order. And if it were entirely up to us, we could not fulfill that response-ability. But it's not entirely up to us! Remember? Christ not only commands: "Follow me" and "Love one another." He also promises: "Lo, I am with you always, to the close of the age."

It is Jesus Christ, our risen Lord, who invites us to this table, not because we are worthy, not because we, with all our human frailties, are able to respond—but because he bids us come, because he promises to be with us. We come to this table to renew our commitment, our pledge of allegiance to Christ and to his church. Yet there are times for each of us when we are not able to renew that pledge— when our thoughts are elsewhere, when our pain seems too great, when we feel only hopelessness or alienation. But *every* time we come to this table, these words are spoken: "This is my body that is broken for you. This cup is the new covenant in my blood." *Every* time we come to this table, Christ is renewing his pledge to us.

As we celebrate the Lord's Supper, remember the promise of Christ's presence now and in the days to come. It is he who sets this table. He offers us not only bread and wine. He offers us forgiveness and wholeness, life and hope, if we will accept his invitation.

SUGGESTIONS FOR WORSHIP

Call to Worship (from Psalm 116:16*a*, 17-19)

LEADER: O Lord, I am your servant. I will offer to you a thanksgiving sacrifice and call on the name of the Lord.
PEOPLE: **I will pay my vows to the Lord in the presence of all God's people, in the courts of the house of the Lord, in your midst, O Jerusalem.**
ALL: **Praise the Lord!**

Assurance of Pardon (adapted from John 3:16-17)

"For God so loved the world that he gave his only son, so that everyone who believes in him may not perish but may have eternal life. Indeed, God did not send the son into the world to condemn the world, but in order that the world might be saved through him."

Friends, believe the good news of God's saving love: In Jesus Christ, you are forgiven.

Good Friday

Jan Fuller Carruthers

Isaiah 52:13–53:12: Isaiah foretells the coming of the Suffering Servant who will bear the sin of many.

Psalm 22: Despite suffering and a sense of abandonment, the psalmist realizes that God is the source of deliverance.

Hebrews 10:16-25: The blood of Jesus, our "great priest," confirms God's promises to us.

John 18:1–19:42: The story of Jesus' arrest, crucifixion, and burial.

REFLECTIONS

The howling agony of Psalm 22 falls, in contextual order, between a glorious song of God's power and might (Psalm 21) and the familiar and tender statement of security, comfort, and rest that is Psalm 23. Already we perceive that these community prayers acknowledge the widest array of the vicissitudes of human life and faith, including a devastating sense of God's absence.

On the day Christians relive the passion and death of Jesus—as aurally and visually we follow him through his arrest, trial, betrayal by friends, violence and abuse, crucifixion, death and burial—Scripture offers our own souls' sufferings a home. And this, even before the redemption of that suffering is evident.

In Matthew's and Mark's Gospels Jesus begins the lament of Psalm 22: "My God, my God, why have you forsaken me?" These are not words reserved for Jesus alone—although now paired with John's passion—but for faithful souls in anguished moments. The prayer requires no special holiness, but only the willingness to acknowledge before God—even who seems not to be listening—all of human expe-

90

rience. In lament, Israel enacts God's faithfulness even as it exercises its own by submitting every moment to intimate and trusting relationship with the Holy One. (The powerful liberation of lament prayer came to me through Walter Brueggemann's book, *The Message of the Psalms: A Theological Commentary* [Augsburg Publishing House, 1984], which I read during a lengthy illness. I recommend it.) We might aspire to such honest exchange, even—especially—as we follow a suffering Savior.

It will be tempting to jump ahead to the glories of Easter's resurrection, depending on a happy ending to protect us from the blinding pain of Good Friday's moment, and our own. But Easter joy takes root in, and depends on, this sustained experience of the grief-stricken mystery of our Lord's death offering. Afterwards, and not without this essential piece, the depth and breadth of new life in Christ will genuinely astound and lift us.

A SERMON BRIEF

Have you ever felt abandoned by God? Tell the truth!

In my early twenties, as a young teacher on mission, I was caught in artillery crossfire in Southern Lebanon during the civil war. Alone for days through the smoking, slamming terror, I wrote with a bitten pencil into a journal. First came words of worry, fear, prayer for deliverance and comfort. Then with no relief in sight, I poured out angry, bitter, abandoned words to God and my family. I still remember with flushing heat the hounding emptiness, the crisis of God's impotence, silence, or unconcern with evil and those in its path. Did God know where I was? Sometimes I am reminded of these feelings in the death of a loved one, when God seems distant, far removed from real human anguish. Later, in saner and safer moments, I razor cut the shaming portions from the book's spine and burned them.

We cover up suffering in our culture, hiding angst or misery. Anne Lamott describes the rules of life. I think you'll recognize them: "you must not have anything wrong with you . . . if you do have something wrong with you, you must get over it as soon as possible . . . if you can't get over it, you must pretend that you have . . . if you can't even pretend . . . you shouldn't show up . . . if you are going to insist on showing up, you should at least have the decency to feel ashamed."[1]

The church hides suffering, too. It is the last place we would admit to feeling hurt or forsaken; surely, any alienation from God would demonstrate only our lack of faith. Church is a place to be on one's best behavior, to think, act, and believe "right." Perhaps worship in particular, and religion in general, is a departure from the "real world," distant from the harsh realities of human living. Today is different. The suffering of the world and the suffering of our Savior are present for all to see and hear. We are meant to live with them with unaverted eyes. Today suffering is uncovered.

Days after the national and global tragedies of September 11, 2001, one of my students confessed, "This is the worst thing that ever happened to me, and nothing happened to me." In sighs and tears, she carried a weight for those to whom it really did happen. In the awful and tender acceptance of human suffering is the spirit of the crucified Jesus alive and well.

Jesus' death is our hope. Humans, being what we are, cannot love God and others the way we are meant to do. The result of this sinfulness would be such distance from God that we would be obliterated by it. The Beloved shouldered the pain, paid the cost of our return to relationship. The distance destroyed him instead of us. Alienation was our sin. God absorbed it in forgiveness and new life, and gave us back our lives in God's presence.

All that we might suffer, Christ absorbed in agony on the cross. It is eternally part of God's memory. Every pain has potential to draw us closer to God, to serve the Holy One, to deliver us back into the lap of love. We may—we must—experience Jesus' pain and suffering on this day. God did not flee from our pain, but felt it, feels it, remembers it, takes it on still, carries it and us. On Good Friday what has been covered is uncovered. The pain of living and dying, mourning, seeking, finding, and not finding is real. It is real on Jesus' head. It is real in God's heart.

The good news is this: The worst thing that ever happened to Jesus happened not to him but to us. It was ours. He took it for us, shouldered and left it at the farthest edge of hell. We need not die from it. Now he remembers with us, in tenderness, sighs, and tears. We remember with him.

What, then, does it mean to follow Christ? Perhaps it is to honestly uncover the pain of life, for all to see, because it is a holy reminder of our salvation. Perhaps it is to feel for others, to willingly take on pain that doesn't belong to us. (I am not here speaking of abusive pain that others make us bear.) Christian compassion knows that the worst thing that happened to me, didn't happen to me, but happened to our human community, to our Savior, to our God. Jesus is the way that God loved the world. Real love feels pain for others, and is not afraid. We need no longer fear our own experience, even of abandonment. All has been redeemed by the wounded shoulders of Jesus.

As of today, we may say every, any, word to God, in whose heart all will be recognized. Thus, the speaking, the living, will lead us directly into the heart of God where the memory of Jesus' suffering resides. There is no victory in denial. We only survive if we pass *through* the days of pain. Only there we will be taught to sing the genuine praises of those who have been abandoned and rescued. We may willingly engage our pains, and those of others, in God's arms. We need not seek out suffering, but live in open and transparent faithfulness.

Today, of all days, do not fear the heights or depths of human experience. On this awesome day, we uncover the reality of what it means to be human, for Jesus and for us. Our own pain and loss cry out and bind us to Jesus in his death. All we are, all we feel, all we need, are here on the cross. Stare in wonder. Adore. Remember and hope. Do not look away.

SUGGESTIONS FOR WORSHIP

Call to Worship

As the crowds were appalled on seeing him
—so disfigured did he look
that he seemed no longer human—
so will the crowds be astonished at him,
and kings stand speechless before him;
for they shall see something never heard before.
(Isaiah 52:14–53:1 JB)

My friends, of all days
This is the one
To look upon wretched death
To perceive our signs of life,
To cease grasping at life,
But to wait for the living.
Come, see, know, and worship.

Call to Confession and Assurance of Pardon

Let us open ourselves to the loving gaze of God as we pray. (Silence.)
Holy and Mighty God,
Before the mystery of your inconceivable love
We fall to our knees in trembling awe
Bewildered and gifted children,
Wretched, unable, tough.
We cry to you from our own depths:
Forgive us for who we are and are not,
For what we do and do not,
For the ways we love and do not love.
Lord, have mercy.
Christ, have mercy.
Lord have mercy.

Assurance of Pardon

The Holy Spirit bears witness to us, saying,
"This is the covenant that I will make with them says the Lord:
I will put my laws on their hearts,
And write them on their minds,
I will remember their sins and their misdeeds no more."

(Hebrews 10:16-17 RSV)

Your sins are forgiven. Live, and love, as new people. Amen.

1. Anne Lamott, *Operating Instructions: A Journal of My Son's First Year* (New York: Pantheon Books, 1993), 100.

Easter Day

Dusty Kenyon Fiedler

Isaiah 65:17-25: The prophet proclaims the wonderful promise that God "is about to create Jerusalem as a joy, and its people as a delight," with the closing image of the wolf and the lamb feeding together.

Psalm 118:1-2, 14-24: The psalmist's refrain, "God's steadfast love endures forever!" is echoed in the shout of victory and the declaration of salvation that God gives, so that all can "rejoice and be glad" in this day!

Acts 10:34-43: Before Cornelius and friends, Peter testifies to the grace of Christ's life and death and resurrection and to God's power through Christ to forgive sins and offer new life.

Luke 24:1-12: In his resurrection account, Luke tells how "the women" go to the tomb and are amazed to find the stone rolled away and the tomb empty. The good news of the resurrection is proclaimed by "two men in dazzling clothes," but the gathered disciples do not believe the amazing news the women share. Peter goes to see for himself.

REFLECTIONS

The more Easter sermons I share with congregations, the more I pay attention to and am amazed by the *loud* voice of the women on Easter Sunday! They play such a central role on this great day. Especially in Luke's account, the unnamed women of verse 1 are given more identity in verse 10 (three of them are named now), and then they stand in such stark contrast to the other disciples who declare the women's good news about the empty tomb to be "an idle tale" (NRSV) or outright "nonsense" (TEV). Most of us, I think, side with these women—we *want* their message

95

to be heard, to be believed, because then we can also celebrate on this Easter Day our own improbable, amazing-grace hopes. If what the women report is true, then we can dare to believe what seems utterly unbelievable—like Isaiah's picture of the new Jerusalem (65:17-25), where there will be no more weeping, or hurting, or destroying, and where all children will be blessed by God with long and fulfilling lives—WOW! But—still, today—this good news Easter message seems more a whisper than a shout of joy. And there are so many barriers and powers that appear to be strong enough to squelch this good news report, because it is too incredible and upsets the status quo—barriers like the smug disbelief of the disciples that *appears* to kill the report and keep these women in their place. (For those of us who have heard and preached so many Easter sermons, one of the strongest barriers to belief may be ho-hum complacency.) But somehow, by God's power, the women prevail! Their message *does* get through. And life is changed—forever.

A SERMON BRIEF

Sometimes I wonder if we don't really *prefer* bad news to good. The biggest newspaper headlines I can remember were tragic—the September 11 attacks, or the assassination of John F. Kennedy, or the death of Princess Diana, or the beginning of the Persian Gulf War. Even our church prayer chains seem to get activated more quickly for tragic needs than for happy thanksgivings. Why is that?

Could it be because bad news doesn't change us as much as good news does? Bad news is easier to fit into our familiar, everyday experiences—it's what we've come to expect from life. Good news, on the other hand, is what we hope for, what we long to hear, but it often requires a "leap of faith," a willingness to believe what we have not seen with our own eyes. Good news can transform us and everything we know, but sometimes we're not quite ready for it.

Luke's account of Jesus' resurrection tells how this most wonderful good news of all almost didn't get through. The women come to the tomb fully expecting to use their spices to prepare Christ's body for burial. The bad news of Jesus' death had rallied them to action, just as the word of a friend's death moves people to action today. These women were faithful and loving followers, fully aware of what the reality of death now required them to do. They fall into their comfortable roles as they come with the necessary burial spices. Probably their conversation on that early morning hike was very practical: Do we have all the needed supplies? What if there are Roman guards at the tomb? How can we roll the heavy stone away? When they arrive, they see that the stone has already been removed. What luck! But, entering the tomb, they are "perplexed" to find no body. What could this empty tomb mean? *Never* had they expected this turn of events. But before the women can deal with this new development, they are surprised by the sudden appearance of two men "in dazzling clothes," and the women cower in great fear. Now they expect the worst—but what could possibly be worse than watching Jesus die on the cross? Somehow, despite their great fear, they hear the *good* news that the men declare: "Why do you look for the living among the dead? He is not here, but has risen" (v. 5*b*). They are reminded of Jesus' own words about his death and power to rise again to new life. And, amazingly, they believe it! They are grasped by good news, and now they see the whole world differently. "Happy are you who weep now; you will laugh!" (Luke 6:21 TEV) Jesus had promised. At the time, they couldn't see how that could ever be true—until now! And "Love your enemies, do good to those who hate you, bless those who curse you, and pray for those who mistreat you" (6:27-28 TEV) had seemed an impossible ethic—until now!

This Easter Day brings us the shocking gift of good news as well: a whole new insight that lifts us out of our old ruts and turns us around so that we can see everything from a shining new perspective. That's why we are here, isn't it? Because in the face of tragedy and difficulty, when our lives get messy or out-of-control, as we struggle with seen and unseen trials, we *want* so much to see and believe that darkness is *not* more powerful than the light, and that Christ's resurrection power *can* transform our lives too. You have to read between the lines to see how this news transforms the women at the empty tomb, but I imagine them giving high-fives and shouting for joy! You just can't take in this amazing announcement without some rejoicing—right? That's why we need trumpets in church on Easter Sunday—to wake us up and maybe even get us on our feet, dancing! For we have the *only* news that can set things to the right—and the world needs to hear it!

But the powers-that-be want nothing of it. An "idle tale" is what the cloistered disciples call this news, and they will not believe it. They choose to stay overwhelmed by the bad news of Christ's death. I expect the women are not surprised, accustomed as they are to their marginalized role. No doubt they understand how easy it is to say "No!" when the day offers us a life-changing "Yes!" But—now they are empowered! These women had not lifted themselves out of their sorrow. God's Easter power has met them unexpectedly at the empty tomb, and God's great Easter victory has transformed all other realities of their lives.

Easter joy like theirs is contagious, and it will not be silenced. That's why Peter gets up, runs to the tomb—and returns, now an amazed believer himself! The good news of Easter is real even in the face of doubt and unbelief; God's living power encounters *us* today. Let us go, like the faithful women, to proclaim this amazing good news!

SUGGESTIONS FOR WORSHIP

Call to Worship

LEADER: This is the day that the Lord has made; let us rejoice and be glad in it! (Psalm 118:24)

PEOPLE: **Indeed we shall rejoice, for Christ our Lord is risen!**

LEADER: Our hearts are glad, O God, for Your power is stronger than anything we have to fear.

ALL: **Alleluia! Christ is risen, indeed!**

Prayer of Confession

Gracious God, We come before you to confess that we are like the other disciples who could not believe the women's amazing good news of the empty tomb, for we go on living our daily lives as if death and powerful foes and evil ways can have their grip on us. Forgive us for not living like Easter people, great God. Empower us for new life that changes everything. Help us to share joyfully as new creations in your love. (Silent prayers of confession) In the name of Jesus we pray. Amen.

Assurance of Pardon

LEADER: Dear Friends, Christ is risen, and God's resurrection power makes us new creations!

PEOPLE: **Thanks be to God, for wiping clean our sinful ways and re-creating us for love!**

ALL: **Alleluia! Our sins are forgiven! We are Easter people!**

Benediction

Go in peace, and may the joyful assurance of God's resurrection power go with you, today and always!

Second Sunday of Easter

Sue A. Ebersberger

Acts 5:27-32: Peter and the apostles defend themselves before the council for teaching in Jesus' name: "We must obey God rather than any human authority."

Psalm 150: This final psalm in the psalter is a hymn of praise: "Let everything that breathes praise the Lord!"

Revelation 1:4-8: John writes an introductory greeting to the seven churches addressed in the book of Revelation by attesting to the grace and peace of Jesus Christ.

John 20:19-31: The risen Jesus mysteriously visits the disciples and equips them with the Holy Spirit. Thomas, who was not present, insists that he will not believe until he has touched Jesus' wounds. Upon doing so, Thomas proclaims "my Lord and my God!"

REFLECTIONS

Things had gone all wrong. Jesus, their Lord and Savior, had been crucified—and with his crucifixion, all their hopes and courage were dashed! But that morning Mary came running from the tomb saying, "He is alive! He called me by name!" But the disciples didn't believe.

In both John and Luke, Jesus was suddenly standing in the midst of the disciples who were gathered together. (Luke implies the disciples thought they were seeing a ghost.) "Peace be with you," Jesus reassures them, and then shows them his hands and side. With that, the disciples recognize the crucified Jesus as the Risen Lord.

Jesus greets them once again—"Peace be with you." This time they recognize the fulfillment of his farewell promises. Jesus commissions the disciples to continue God's work and equips them with the Holy Spirit.

Thomas, who was not present, states his skepticism. He lays out *his* conditions of faith. "To believe, I must touch the holes left from the nails driven into my Lord's hands. I must feel the gaping hole in his side." Thomas essentially asks for the same "proof" that Jesus has already given the rest of the disciples.

Jesus comes again to the disciples—this time when Thomas is present. Jesus graciously offers to meet Thomas's conditions. "Do not be unbelieving, but believing" Jesus urges Thomas. With that, Thomas makes one of the most powerful testimonials in the book of John to Jesus' divinity: "My Lord and my God."

Amid the many possibilities for a sermon, I was drawn to the deep connection between Thomas and Jesus. I wanted the congregation to feel the powerful personal connection that was created between the two when Thomas touched Jesus' wounds. In touching the wounds of Jesus, Jesus became the "real" risen Christ to Thomas. When we touch each other's wounds, we also become "real" to one another. In becoming "real," we become God's creation complete with knicks, cuts, and scratches. And in that connection, we truly become Christ's body and blood in the world for one another.

A SERMON BRIEF

My three-year-old daughter, Grace, came home with a long, convoluted tale one day. She began by saying "That's it! You're in 'time out' for being too rowdy!" Well, I was a bit confused because I rarely use "time out" and have never used it for her being "rowdy." So I asked her, "Were you put in time out at school today?" Suddenly a long tale about the bad boys who pushed her, followed by the description of a redheaded little boy who pinched her, ended in confession. "I hit Sam today."

"Oh," I said, wondering what to do or say next and thinking, "This is my beautiful baby girl whom I want to be kind to everyone." "And why did you hit Sam?" I asked. "Because he was standing next to me, and I told him to move and he didn't." "Hmmmm." I responded. Her words got caught on themselves as she told me how Sam cried and wouldn't stop crying. "I hurt his feelings," the confession tumbled out at last. Woundedness begins at such a young age!

Thomas carried his own wounds! Earlier in the book of John,

Thomas speaks courageously—encouraging the disciples to follow Jesus, even unto death (John 11:16). And yet, when push came to shove, Thomas deserted Jesus along with everyone else. So here he was, hearing stories of how Jesus had come to all the other disciples, showing them his wounds. And I'll bet he wondered why he was always out when the important things happened.

Perhaps Thomas's conscience wiggled a bit, but not quite enough for a confession. Instead, Thomas insists that he must see Jesus' wounds with his own eyes to truly believe that Jesus had risen. But seeing them was not enough to believe. Thomas knows he must *feel* the nail marks in Jesus' hands.

Jesus suddenly appears again to the disciples. This time, it's Thomas he wants to see! "Come here, Thomas. Touch the raw wounds left by the nail marks. See the oozing of the blood on my side. Do what you need to do to believe." Can't you just imagine Thomas tentatively reaching up with his finger, unsure of what he would find if he moved any closer. Was this a mirage? A ghost? Or could it *be* the Risen Lord?

During this exchange, a deep and powerful connection is made between the two. In touching the wounds of Jesus, Jesus became the "real" risen Christ to Thomas. "My Lord and my God!" was Thomas's emphatic response.

When we allow someone to touch our wounds, we too become "real" to one another. Take Mary for example. Mary put up electric fences around herself—ready to shock anyone who got too close with a charge of anger! You could almost watch groups of people part to move away when she tried to join them.

One day, I was sitting with Mary during a potluck dinner. She had told me before about the many trips she had taken her children on as they were growing up. In the past, she had always presented these trips in a lighthearted way, telling of all the fun and laughter they had shared as a family. But on this particular evening, Mary looked me straight in the eye and said, "Do you know why I took my children on all those trips?" "No," I replied. "Because my husband was having an affair; in fact, he had a child by that woman. Every time something awful would happen, like when his other child was born, or he thought he might like to 'give it a go' with 'her,' I decided that it would cost him. So I took our children on trips." It was as if Mary looked at me and said, "Look at the nail marks on my soul." With that, all the distance that I put between us because of her anger fell away. Wounds make for deep and genuine connections.

The nail marks on our hands come from betrayals of covenants, seeing the terrors of violence, or having a child born with a severe disability. The gaping hole in our side is torn wide open by harsh words and acts of indifference. But in sharing our wounds, we become God's creation—complete with knicks, cuts and scratches. We become Christ's body and blood in the world for one another. Our willingness to share the messiness of our wounds with another allows the wounds to be resurrected into something new—something better.

SUGGESTIONS FOR WORSHIP

Call to Worship

LEADER: We come this morning to find a life shaped by joy!

PEOPLE: We come this morning to find a life grounded in Jesus' peace!

LEADER: We gather this morning to be guided by the Holy Spirit.

ALL: We gather together to worship our Risen Lord, Jesus Christ! Thanks be to God!

Prayer of Confession and Assurance of Pardon

Gracious God, we come this morning filled with fear and trembling. Sometimes we don't want to believe unless we can put our hands in your wounds. Sometimes we don't want to feel other people's wounds because we may get too close—we may care too much.

Help us believe before touching wounds. Move us to compassion for everyone. Give us courage to share our own sore spots with others and to be willing to connect deeply with one another. Amen.

LEADER: Friends, the eyes of Christ are upon you. Hear Christ say to you, "Put your finger here and see my hands. Reach out your hand and put it in my side. Do not be faithless but believing." Touch the wounds of Christ and believe the good news of the gospel: in Jesus Christ you are healed and forgiven.

Benediction (adapted from Revelation 1:5-6)

Go out in the name of the One who loves us and freed us from our sins by his blood and made us to be a kingdom. To him be glory and dominion forever and ever.

Third Sunday of Easter

Wanda Burton-Crutchfield

Acts 9:1-6 (7-20): The ultimate conversion story of Saul begins with deep anger, climaxes with being struck by a cosmic light, and ends with that scene that births beautiful metaphors, the scales falling from Saul's eyes.

Psalm 30: Words that must be sung—"You have turned my mourning into dancing"—surely contain the reason we celebrate God. God has chosen to love us.

Revelation 5:11-14: God's plan comes to completion as God's ultimate emissary receives full power and authority. Every creature joins in song, celebrating the coming victory.

John 21:1-19: Just as seven disciples have returned to their former profession following Jesus' death, Jesus makes his third resurrection appearance. The disciples are brought back into service, blessed with a *Eucharist* meal, and commanded by Jesus to "Follow me."

REFLECTIONS

A dear friend of mine, Dr. Philip M. Young, is a gifted composer of sacred music. I was fortunate enough to be a member of his choir as a recording of his compositions was made. One of the songs, adapted from Psalm 30, holds an amazing energy. The song echoes the psalm as it begins with a steady, forceful beat, praising God. But it bursts into a surprise, a lilting waltz, at the conclusion of the psalm when our laments are turned into dancing, our sackcloth is removed, and God has "clothed (us) with joy" (30:11).

A special excitement stirred in Phil as he prepared his choir. Most of the folk with him in the room had shared a good portion of his forty-plus years as minister to First Baptist Church, Henderson, North Carolina. From his arrival as a youngster fresh from graduate school with his equally talented, musical collaborator wife, Mary Lou, to his grief at losing her to cancer, this choir had been with him. As Phil spoke about the music we were preparing to sing one night, he offered how true the words of the psalmist are. Laments do turn into dancing. Phil was about to walk down the aisle once again to marry his best friend, Sue.

Perhaps the apostle Paul sang this psalm as he danced through the synagogues telling the story of his miraculous call to believe in the love God showed through Jesus. Saul's bitter, passionate anger becomes Paul's tremendous joy in a burst of light on a Damascus road.

It is the song of Easter. Though a congregation may have heard this story again and again, like any good music, this song has the capacity to catch the listener off guard. Perhaps there are scales on the eyes of the Christian, almost Christian, and name-only Christian who encounter this story in Eastertide.

A SERMON BRIEF

I knew a man once who had a problem. He was a minister with four kids and a wife and a cat named Percy. Percy was a fighting tomcat. Every few months or so, the moon would be just right, and Percy would throw himself wholeheartedly into a solid midnight rumble. The man would watch his cat return, bleeding, ears torn, eyes scratched, limping, but self-satisfied—Percy the Triumphant. Inevitably, Percy would require a veterinarian's care. With four growing children, whose future education mattered and whose present hunger required satisfaction, the man knew that regular veterinarian visits did not fit into the family's budget.

The man had a problem. There were quite a few people who had opinions concerning ways to resolve the problem of Percy, the fighting tom. One friend suggested the man give Percy away. I doubt the friend giving advice ever tried to give away a cat, much less an adult male who like Brando in *On the Waterfront* days, thinks "he coulda been a contendah." Another well-meaning counselor advised the man to drop Percy off in the woods far from home. But of course, the next morning after the drop, the friends decided, even a television psychic could predict who would be waiting on the stoop. The most preposterous suggestion was to shoot old Percy. But that was unthinkable to the man.

The man had a problem and the problem was, he loved Percy. Since he and his family had invited this fighting tom into their hearts, the vet continued to get periodic visits, the man anguished over what should be done, and Percy stayed a regular in the local midnight matches. The man's problem was that he loved Percy.

In that familiar conversion story of Saul becoming Paul found in Acts chapter 9, we see that God had a problem as well. God loved Saul.

Saul seems perfectly suited for a black hat as the chapter opens. We are already familiar with the work of this particular fighting tom: the young man who held the coats for those who stoned Stephen, the one inspired by this act enough to drag men and women out of their homes to be thrown into prison, and the one fired up in his quest against Jesus' followers enough to be commissioned by the high priest to bring them bound back to Jerusalem. Saul is bitterly angry as the story of his conversion begins in Acts. He has murder in his eyes.

But God loves this passionate firebrand that only God could figure would become the church's greatest missionary. On the way to the synagogues of Damascus, Saul encounters a heavenly light that sparks all around him. Like the call of Moses, the divine speaks from the light. The one commissioned in God's name to murder followers of Christ now encounters the risen Christ himself. Saul is sent to the city by Jesus this time, rather than by the high priest. Saul's eyes once filled with rage now see nothing. For three days he sits, eating nothing, thinking, and waiting.

By the time God convinces the disciple Ananias to visit Saul, lay hands on him, and share with him the gospel, Saul is ready. As the Holy Spirit is welcomed into the heart of Saul, eyes filled with rage and then blinded by God are ready to lose their scales. God knew that this problem could be an instrument of joy.

The words of Psalm 30 spring to mind as we read of Paul going from synagogue to synagogue praising God and preaching the gospel. Rage, which masked emptiness and pain, is turned to joy. Lament becomes a dance.

God has a problem, today. The problem is that God loves us. We claim to believe the story of Easter that Jesus rose from the dead so that we might understand love. But how often does praise burst forth from our beings in songs? We drag ourselves to the door, exhausted and torn from our catfights; but we would rather do battle than be lifted to joy by God. We are better at plowing through life on a mission than letting ourselves go enough to be captivated by unimaginable love. The song of Easter is one that melts the heart, sets toes to tapping, makes bodies sway, inspires us to love, and compels us to share in it.

Do you ever wonder what might have happened if Saul had stayed Saul, nursed his anger, and kept the scales over his eyes? There might be quite a few fewer epistles to read and quite a few fewer people to read them.

We are called to be Easter people; we are called to celebrate a risen Lord. This joy should be so strong it captivates all of who we are. The incongruity of the love that God has for us should bring us to the ground just as Saul was bowed by Christ's presence. But then that same love raises us to dance and sing. Our sackcloths become baptismal garments of joy. Christ is love. Christ is raised from the dead. Alleluia. Amen.

SUGGESTIONS FOR WORSHIP

Call to Worship (inspired by John 20–21)

ONE: The tomb is empty. Where is the risen Lord?
MANY: **Jesus is comforting a woman who thinks all is lost.**
ONE: The tomb is empty. Where is the risen Lord?
MANY: **Jesus is visiting the ones who are locked behind the doors of fear. They are scared of what might happen.**
ONE: The tomb is empty. Where is the risen Lord?
MANY: **Jesus is feeding the ones he needs to follow him. Jesus is teaching them how to feed his sheep.**
ONE: The tomb is empty. Where is the risen Lord?
MANY: **Jesus is here, comforting us, bringing us peace, feeding us, and calling us to the dance of discipleship.**
ONE: The tomb is empty. Let us celebrate together.

Prayers of the People

ONE: What petitions would you bring to the risen Lord? What pain keeps you weeping through the night?

What anger keeps you from casting off your sackcloth for clothing of joy? The Lamb upon the throne is mighty enough to hear what is on our hearts, take what is binding us, and heal what is stilling us. Let us pray.

MANY: **O God, we enter your throne room this day, blinded by the light of your truth and beauty. Our beings are not ready to be lifted to the heights of joy you have for us. We are concerned for family and friends who do not know your love. We weep at the ways we humans treat one another and the world. We wonder what it is that you want from us. Please loose that which binds us. Heal minds too clouded to sing; inspire our spirits to dance. And may we proclaim with all of creation: "Worthy is the Lamb." To you be "blessing and honor and glory and might forever and ever!" Amen.**

Benediction

Like Saul, we arrived in this place with bitterness in our hearts. Some of us, like old Percy, were ready for a fight. Jesus has met us on this road and shown us what we can be. Let the scales drop. See your Savior. Leave this place dancing and singing. Amen.

Fourth Sunday of Easter

Kitty Cooper Holtzclaw

Acts 9:36-43: Peter is summoned to Joppa after the death of the widow Tabitha. Peter prays by her deathbed and commands her to "get up." Tabitha awakens to life, bearing witness for all to the power of God at work through the disciples.

Psalm 23: The familiar and beloved "shepherd psalm" reminds us of God's persistent presence and care.

Revelation 7:9-17: A diverse multitude of people, those who have survived "the great ordeal," bow down to worship the Lamb.

John 10:22-30: Jesus declares that he knows his sheep, those who follow him, and will forever care for them.

REFLECTIONS

Being this deep in the season of Easter presents a struggle for me each year. I want to keep the focus on Easter rather than jumping ahead to Pentecost, but my thoughts on resurrection seem stale. By this point, I have already been through the historical aspects of resurrection and the resurrection of Jesus Christ and even the aspects of resurrection in our lives. It is time to make resurrection manifest, but taking that too far can take the fresh wind out of Pentecost. So in this particular sermon, I chose to focus on the deep impact our lives can have in the world because we are followers of the risen Christ.

A SERMON BRIEF

Deep Impact

The birth of my younger brother.
My first day of first grade.

The death of my grandmother, then my grandfather.
Puberty.
Going to college.
Falling in love.
Becoming a mother.
The *Challenger* explosion.
Hearing my call.
Answering my call.
September 11, 2001.

Some of these events were positive and life-giving. Some were cataclysmic and catastrophic. Some were chosen. Some were unavoidable. Some were private. Some were global. Each of them had a deep impact, for good or bad, on my life. They define and form me as a person. My life would be different without any one of them and vastly different without all of them.

Most days of my life are mundane. Most events of my life cannot be recalled. I don't remember how I spent my thirty-second birthday or Tuesday three weeks ago. If I tried long and hard enough, I could recall some of those lost days; but by and large, I am afraid most are gone from my recollection forever. Despite my forgetting them, they also help make me who I am. Out of the sum of the memorable and unmemorable, I am whoever I am.

I am who I am and you are who you are because of nature and nurture. For all our similarities, you are distinct. No one, even a twin, is exactly like anyone else. We may think that everybody else thinks like we do—or if they don't, they should. Everyone should have tastes similar to ours. If they don't, they should strive for them. At the same time, we yearn to be unique in the world.

But to observe our daily lives, we are not so very different from each other. If we followed each other around for days at a time, we wouldn't observe many differences. We all go to the grocery store and to the pharmacy. We travel in vehicles to get from place to place. Most of us eat three meals a day. At certain ages, we entertain similar habits. Each day we follow similar cycles of work, rest, and refreshment. All in all, we are not very different from the other three thousand or so that gather within these walls to worship. From outward appearance, we are not very different from other denominations worshiping on Sunday mornings. Our lives are not outwardly very different from those who claim no faith in Jesus Christ.

Considering our lives from this perspective is discouraging. Are we ineffective as Christians and unimportant as persons? Are we no more than ants scurrying in and out of the anthill?

You know we are. You know it for a fact, and you feel it as a child of God. We know that our lives have more impact than appears on the surface because we feel the effects of what others have done for us. We know we are more than the sum of our parts because we have seen amazing things happen in the lives of others. When God does the adding, sums just don't add up the same as when we alone do. Because God works in our lives, people succeed against great odds. Projects as small as mustard seeds grow and grow until they give shelter and comfort and food to many. These kinds of things happen because we have faith in the risen Christ, and his resurrection gives life to us.

One of the defining questions of our lives is, "What do you want people to say at your funeral?" Perhaps the better question is, "What do you want people to say while they are standing in the line waiting for the fried chicken and potato salad the church will serve your family before your funeral?" That is when more truth is told. That is when we will hear the real stories of who you were. I remember a parishioner saying, "All this church needs to grow is a few good funerals." How sad! How funny! How often true. Other than our immediate families, who will grieve for us? Will anyone be relieved that we have gone to our—um—reward?

Acts gives us the funeral scenario we should all strive for. Tabitha had died. The obituary was sketchy. Was she young? Old? Rich? Poor? We know very little. But we know that her life made a deep impact in her community because of her generosity. She was devoted to good works and acts of charity. The widows (hear that as the poor, those who had no one to provide for them) were weeping and showing Peter the tunics Tabitha had made for them. She had her priorities in godly order and lived her life out of that order. She did this because she followed the teachings of her Master, the Lord Jesus Christ.

Because of her life and faith, many had been blessed and many were brought into the circle called the church. Because she lived the teachings of the Giver of Life, many others experienced new life. The impact her death had on the community was deep because of the seemingly small things she did in her life.

Tabitha.

Peter.

Albert Einstein.

My third grade teacher.

Alexander the Great.

Martin Luther King, Jr.

The boy who rescued the kitten from the street.
Johann Sebastian Bach.

All of these individuals had a deep impact in the world. All of them have died or will die one day. So will you. Will you avail the days of your life to teachings of Jesus Christ and use your days for the glory of his kingdom?

SUGGESTIONS FOR WORSHIP

Call to Worship

LEADER: Get up, sons and daughters of God!
PEOPLE: **God revives and restores us.**
LEADER: The Good Shepherd goes with us through even the darkest places.
PEOPLE: **We do not fear because we receive God's comfort.**
LEADER: Surely goodness and mercy shall follow us all the days of our lives.
PEOPLE: **We will follow pathways of goodness to the places our Lord leads us.**

Prayer of Confession

God of heaven and earth, we need your compassion. We work, trying to earn respect. We strive, trying to achieve more and more. Yet, with all our best efforts, we fall short. We do not see the fruits of our labors, even those with the best intentions. We grieve the loss of our sacrifices when we have so much more than others.

We are foolish and vain and frail. Through your salvation make us wise and humble and strong in you. We fall on our faces acknowledging our sin. Wash our sin-stained robes and make us new. Amen.

Assurance of Pardon

LEADER: Salvation belongs to God who freely offers it to any who would accept it.
PEOPLE: **Blessing and glory be to God.**
LEADER: Receive the forgiveness of sins.
PEOPLE: **Wisdom and thanksgiving be to God.**
LEADER: Worship God day and night.

PEOPLE: **Honor and power and might be to our God forever and ever! Amen.**

Benediction

Go forward from this place and be known as people of good works and acts of charity. God wants us to change the world. Trust in Eternal Strength for this life and the next. Amen.

Fifth Sunday of Easter

Helen Nablo

Acts 11:1-18: Peter reports the activities of the disciples to the church in Jerusalem.

Psalm 148: This psalm calls all of creation to join in praising God.

Revelation 21:1-6: The vision of the new heaven and the new earth.

John 13:31-35: After washing the disciples' feet, Jesus commands them to "love one another" following the example of his love for them.

REFLECTIONS

The text from Revelation, surely many people's favorite passage from that book, is a good balance for the notion of a rapture where people will be taken up into heaven at an appointed hour. Here, a heavenly city descends from heaven down to earth. Here, God comes down to earth to take up residence among us.

If one were preaching this text at a healing service, it would be fitting to focus on the vision of healing and wholeness that comes with God's residence among us—no more suffering, death, or mourning. But what is also striking are the words of the one on the throne when all this comes to pass. After proclaiming that all things are being made new, a promise is made: "To the thirsty I will give water as a gift from the spring of the water of life."

There is an economic contrast in those words about water, a contrast between God's political economy and the present order of the Roman Empire—or of our empire for that matter. Because we know so much about our economy, this world of Madison Avenue and the economic survival of the fittest, we don't really know that much about a reality where water—or anything else—is given without price. The question that formed for me, the question I hope the sermon will address, is this: What would it be like to live in a world so different from ours, a world where grace and the things needful for life come freely, without price?

A SERMON BRIEF

Free Water

Summer was drawing close and so "Squirrel Hill Days," the neighborhood celebration, was right around the corner. Situated on a central corner at a busy intersection of that part of the city, the church I was serving wanted to think about how we might participate that year. After all, it was an opportunity to reach out, to make our strong but somewhat reticent church better known.

Thus, in true Presbyterian fashion, a planning meeting was held. A time to brainstorm how we might get involved. We thought about having church brochures set up on a table, about opening up the building for tours of the tower. We thought about having some kind of children's entertainment—maybe a storyteller or a clown—out on the little patch of lawn in front of the church. As these many thoughts were being tossed about, Steve, the seminarian, said, "I know this sounds rather simple, but why don't we just give out free water? It will likely be a hot day, and that just might be what people really need the most." Well, it took a few moments for the people in the group to let go of their ideas enough to consider this; but after a time, we were soon in agreement. I remember thinking, "This might be kind of silly," but, well, the committee had decided: Free water it would be.

A few weeks later the big day came. And sure enough it *was* a hot day, very hot. Several church members staffed a table with big plastic jugs of water and copious amounts of paper cups. When people saw the banner proclaiming "Free Water" they came up the steps, looking eager and thankful. All day long, water was given out—with a smile, sometimes with a prolonged conversation.

For something I had thought might be silly, it was truly amazing. There in the middle of all the sidewalk sales and hotdog vendors was the church—offering something that was genuinely free. Something only to be received, whoever you were. Those handing out the water were amazed at the gratitude expressed for such a simple gift. They were also amazed at what a privilege it was to be there, handing out the water. Somehow that simple gift spoke more for the church and the gospel of Jesus Christ than a hundred banners or a thousand brochures ever could. Cups of water and smiles spoke volumes about the amazing grace of God.

The whole thing made me realize something new about John's vision of a new heaven and earth, and something new about our present life. John's vision of the redeemed city, like the day of free water, goes completely against what we are used to. For us, there is so little in life that doesn't cost us something, that is not handed to us with a set of expectations, a prior motive, that when we receive such graceful giving, we are truly amazed. We live in a world of debt and debt obligations, a world of privilege leading to the rich getting richer, using up more of the resources that are meant for all. The new heaven and earth, the day when God dwells among us wiping every tear from our eyes, will be a new economy, as different as different can be. It will come as a gift to all, but it will also turn the things we have become used to upside down.

That day, our church became a gathering place for the whole neighborhood. Men and women, children and old people, Christians and Jews, pierced and proper, people in all manner of form and dress lingered there. There was something about free water that made folk flock to our steps, our lawn, our church—something about this economy that brought us together in joy, laughter, and gratitude.

And so, remembering our scripture I give thanks. I give thanks for the beautiful vision of Revelation given to us in the pages of our Holy Book. But perhaps even more I give thanks for such an experience in life—the day our church, by the grace of God, had the inspiration and vision to put away our brochures, to do something different—to give out something for free.

SUGGESTIONS FOR WORSHIP

Call to Worship (based on Psalms 148 and 150)

LEADER: Mountains and all hills, fruit trees and all cedars!

PEOPLE: **Kings of the earth and all peoples, princes and rulers of the earth!**

LEADER: Young men and women alike, old and young together!

PEOPLE: **Let us praise the name of the Lord! Let everything that breathes praise the Lord!**

Prayer of Confession

Holy God, we confess
that our ways our not your ways.
You offer us grace and visions of abundant life,
but we live judging others, counting the cost of everything.
Clinging to old ways, we fail to reflect the new things you are doing.
Forgive us and renew us.
Reshape us in the image
of the new heaven and earth that you promise will one day come,
that we might live more hopefully, more faithfully, more joyfully.
We ask this in the strong and sure name of your Son, Jesus Christ.
Amen.

Assurance of Pardon

Anyone who is in Christ is a new creation.
Old things are passing away, and the new has come.
Friends hear and believe the great good news:
In Jesus Christ, we are forgiven.
In Jesus Christ, we are invited to begin again.

Charge and Benediction

In John's Gospel it says,
"Out of the believer's heart shall flow rivers of living water" (John 7:38).
Go now, as God's people in the world
that from your heart
the love of God, the grace of our Lord Jesus Christ,
and the encouragement of the Holy Spirit
shall flow.
Go in peace, to love and serve the Lord.

Sixth Sunday of Easter

Amy Louise Na

Acts 16:9-15: Paul, Silas, and Timothy travel to Europe to spread the gospel. As a result of their testimony, Lydia, a dealer in purple, and her household are baptized.

Psalm 67: A psalm of praise for God's salvation and thanksgiving for the abundance of God's blessing.

Revelation 21:10, 21:22–22:5: John sees the city of Jerusalem inhabited by the Lord. In his vision, the city is transformed into one of light and purity with a living river flowing through it.

John 14:23-29: In response to one of the disciple's questions, Jesus instructs his followers that he will reveal himself to them as they obey his words and as they receive the Holy Spirit.

John 5:1-9: On the Sabbath, near the Sheep Gate, Jesus speaks to the man who had been waiting by the healing pool. Jesus' words take away his thirty-eight-year-old affliction.

REFLECTIONS

In this familiar text, Jesus heals a man he found sitting by the Sheep Gate near a pool of water. According to the local tradition, an angel comes at various times and stirs the water. The first person to step in the recently stirred water is made well. The blind, the lame, the paralyzed, and the diseased are healed in this pool of water. In the text, on this particular day, there is a man, ill for thirty-eight years, who keeps struggling to get into the water. The text never says that he is a paralytic, but we assume he is because he cannot move himself to the pool in time to be healed.

Jesus is there, and, of course, Jesus heals the man. The healing then raises issues and questions about Jesus' authority and identity. The Messiah surely would not heal or do any work on the Sabbath! And, we note, the man himself never displays gratitude or says thank you. He simply obeys Jesus.

This is a story about healing. At the start of the story, healing is an ongoing local tradition. By the end of the story, another healer, Jesus, has entered the scene and sped up the process.

These ideas of suffering and miraculous healing together in the presence of Jesus and water remind me of baptism. In the waters of baptism, we are healed of our infirmities. We are forgiven our sin. We are given new life in Christ, and we, also, often forget or fail to reply with gratitude to the magnitude of this event in our lives. The theme of baptism also fits with the season of Easter, which is about new life and new beginnings. This sermon was preached on a rainy day in a retirement home where the residents celebrated the Lord's Supper.

A SERMON BRIEF

Water and the Word

The act of healing is a mysterious science. Scientists probably thought they had the whole thing figured out with the birth of the antibiotic. But long before the discovery of modern drugs, water played an important part in healing—and continues to do so today. If you've ever visited the Dead Sea, you know its water is thick and dense due to its high salt content. The salt acts as a healer. If you have a cut, the salt-water combination heals the wound, albeit painfully. Other kinds of water also heal, like whirlpool treatments for sprains and torn ligaments. Arthritis and aching bones can be soothed and massaged by the repetitious, warm swirls of water. One new thing in childbirth is a whirlpool or hot tub experience to help ease contractions before delivery. Water therapy is another form of modern medicine that heals.

These modern water therapies would be nothing new to those who sat by the pool at the Sheep Gate in Jerusalem in this familiar Gospel text. This is one of the miracle or healing stories like so many others we find in the New Testament. According to the story, there is a man, ill for thirty-eight years, waiting by the water pool for the angel and his chance to be healed. But he cannot seem to get into the water before another, so he sits on the side. Jesus sees the man lying there, the text says. Jesus asks him, "Do you want to be made well?" The man explains that each time the water is stirred, some one else steps into the pool of water before he can get there. I suppose Jesus takes that answer as a "yes," because next Jesus says to him, "Stand up, take your mat and walk." And the text says that at once, the man was made well.

Now all this occurred on the Sabbath, getting Jesus in trouble with local religious leaders for his healing activity. They were seeking to discover if Jesus was the Messiah, as so many claimed. Jesus' "work" on the Sabbath, coupled with his seeming indifference to Sabbath laws, made the whole idea of his messianic claims seem questionable in the eyes of resident, holy officials. Nevertheless, with his words, Jesus healed the man.

In this short text, in this brief story about a nameless man, his thirty-eight-year affliction, and the casual, yet powerful presence of Jesus Christ, we have a miracle—a healing by water and the word.

The water pool was a local healing spot for the surrounding community. It was a familiar method for healing the devastating illnesses and infirmities of members of the Jerusalem community. The simple act of stepping into the stirred water made the diseased and the lame well again. And the simple words, spoken by Jesus, healed too.

We still see water as a healer. In science and in medicine, its value is considerable. In the church, the waters of baptism are mysterious, but they also convey healing power. Through baptism, the common and ordinary element of water is made into the cleansing waters of new life that unite all believers into one family of God and remind us of God's salvation for God's people.

We also know the healing power of the word. In the reading and the hearing of Scripture, we are reminded of our salvation through Jesus Christ, the Redeemer of all. The word seals the acts of God in Jesus Christ, and we are able to read and hear and proclaim and abide in the word—and the Word—by the grace of God and the power of the Holy Spirit.

The water and the word: both are integral parts of this Gospel text, and both remind us of God's salvation, God's healing, and God's grace and love for us and for all. When it rains, or when you get a shower or wash your hands, remember the healing powers of water. Remember that you are a child of God. Remember your baptism and rejoice in your salvation. When you read God's word, when you hear it proclaimed in a sermon or in a conversation with a friend, rejoice and give thanks that God speaks to you, calling you and claiming you for God's purposes.

Brothers and sisters, in remembering your baptism and in hearing God's word, be healed of your infirmities. Bind yourselves no longer to sinful ways; be freed from the temptations of gossip and impatience and greed. Be healed. Be made whole. Our loving Lord Jesus Christ reminds you again today of his deep love for you and his great desire to be with you. Walk in the power and might of the eternal and mysterious Lord of all. In water and the word, God is revealed and comes to us. In water and the word, God's covenant with us is renewed, the covenant we celebrate at this table. Let the remembrance of our baptism, the words of God's promises, and the sustenance of this meal make us whole and healed and ready to serve the Lord.

SUGGESTIONS FOR WORSHIP

Call to Worship (based on Revelation 21)

LEADER: In the presence of the Lord, the night becomes like day,

PEOPLE: The glory of the Lord shall be our light.

LEADER: All nations, the kings of the earth will know,

PEOPLE: The glory of the Lord shall be our light.

LEADER: In God's presence, all abomination and falsehoods will cease,

PEOPLE: The glory of the Lord shall be our light.

LEADER: In our midst, the river of life flows, giving healing and light.

PEOPLE: The glory of the Lord shall be our light. Let us worship him.

Prayer of Confession (based on Psalm 67)

LEADER: Let us open our hearts to confess our sins, let us pray.

ALL: **Almighty and loving Lord, for this season of hope and salvation, we give you thanks. Forgive us, we pray, for looking past your light and glory into the darkness of our desire and our pride. Forgive the nations and the peoples for their careless acts toward each other. We forget that we are your children scattered throughout the earth. Fill us with**

music and praise so that we may sing of your salvation for us and for all. Bring us into the light of
your presence and reveal your way in our hearts.
Set us on the path of obedience and new life, we
pray in Jesus' name. Amen.

Assurance of Pardon

Brothers and sisters, the saving power of the Lord is known upon
the earth and among all nations. Rejoice and be glad. God has heard
our cries and has answered them with love and compassion. God's
goodness is all around us. Let us bless and praise God's holy name. Be
assured that in Jesus Christ, we are forgiven. Amen.

Ascension of the Lord

Teresa Lockhart Stricklen

Acts 1:1-11: The apostles bear witness to their final conversation with Jesus and his ascension into heaven.

Psalm 47 or Psalm 93: Both psalms declare the reign of God over all nations and all creation.

Ephesians 1:15-23: The writer to the Ephesians confirms Christ's eternal and heavenly rule over all things and every age.

Luke 24:44-53: For the final time, Jesus teaches the disciples, reiterating his mission and commissioning them as witnesses to his words. Then he is received into heaven.

REFLECTIONS

The Ascension is not about Jesus on a backlit elevator cloud being beamed up to God. The early church is borrowing a common apocalyptic motif of resurrection from the dead and ascension to indicate Jesus is Lord, ruling the whole world as divine. Luke's resurrection account stresses Jesus' exaltation. Therefore, we are asked why we seek the living among the dead (24:5-6). Acts 1:11 asks an interesting parallel question: "Why do you stand looking agog into the heavens?" (Somewhere in between is where to look!) As he arose, so he will descend again. There's a redemptive recycling of humanity through the divinity of the human Jesus going on in Luke's divine gift exchange. The following sermon was crafted with this sense of the movement of the theological meaning of the Ascension of Christ and was originally preached to a traditional white, southern, liberal, Presbyterian congregation.

122

A SERMON BRIEF

Earlier this week when I told someone that we would be celebrating Christ's Ascension today, the person asked, "What's with that anyway?" Ascension Day is the day we celebrate the resurrected Christ's exaltation to rule over the whole earth as God. Ascension Day is about worshiping Jesus as God, ruler over the whole earth, Jesus as King of the World![1]

So what? We know Jesus rules. What's the big deal that we need to have a special day to celebrate Jesus as ruler of all? Ascension Day celebrates the essence of the confession of our faith by which we live and die. When we stand to say what it is we believe during our confession of faith, we're saying the most ancient confession of faith: Jesus Christ is Lord. When the early disciples refused to obey the civil authorities and stop preaching about Jesus, they proclaimed Jesus rules. When martyrs refused to bow down to worship the Roman emperor, they sang Jesus Christ is Lord. When church reformers bucked the church's authority, they said Jesus Christ alone is head of the church. When the Reformed church issued the Barmen Declaration in the midst of the Nazi regime, they stared down Hitler to declare Jesus Christ supreme ruler. When Quakers refuse to serve in the armed forces, it's because they believe Jesus Christ, not the military, has ultimate power. When church members endure persecution for taking political justice stances, it's because we believe Jesus Christ rules according to God's Kingdom principles. So what's the big deal? Ascension Day is about Jesus Christ ruling as God, Lord of all. That's so what, and that's everything.

Perhaps now we can see why we've forgotten Ascension Day. We've displaced Jesus as Lord. We've knocked Christ off the throne as if he were a contender for the last musical chair that *we're* determined to get. Without Christ ruling the world, we can seat our own gods. Everyone knows America rules the world. So when following Christ hinders the American way, our nationalism can search Scripture for passages that uphold our capital gains and ignore the Bible's prophetic denouncements that judge us as an unjust society. We knock Christ off the throne to replace him with a flag-draped Bible so our vested interests can rule. Of course Jesus Christ is head of the church. But some days you have to wonder because it sure looks like what really rules the church is whatever faction has the most political power to enable it to scramble onto the throne of God. Surely Jesus still rules the individual hearts of church members—or does he? Consider: When was the last time you went to buy a new house and your Christian realtor said, "You need to buy this less expensive house in a worse neighborhood than you can afford so you'll have enough money to give to the poor?"—and you bought it? Aren't we more likely to stretch to buy the house in the BMW neighborhood than we are to buy the decent house next door to a Mexican-American single mom who drives a Ford Escort? Who cares that it's in an integrated neighborhood that's looking to be revitalized and that we have the gifts needed to help turn things around. We do ministry at the church; we don't want to take God's Kingdom ministry *home* with us. Truth be told, we'd rather have the comfort of doing what we want with our own kind and our own hard-earned money. So from Jesus Christ exalted to rule over all the world, to ruler of the nation, to the head of the church, to the king of hearts, Christ has been shoved off the throne of God into smaller and smaller domains until it seems Christ really isn't ruler of anything anymore; we are. No wonder we'd just as soon forget Ascension Day. We'd rather be God.

Of course, you know there's another way: Reverse. We need to reverse our movement. Instead of bringing Christ down to our level so we can rule, we can raise Christ up so in the humility of our reliance upon his resurrection power, we can be exalted to participate in the very work of God in the world. Why else are we here today in worship? We've come because somewhere deep inside we know we need Christ to save us. We tried doing all the self-help. It didn't work. But when we admitted our need for God, there was transforming power through Jesus Christ who did for us what we could not do for ourselves by humbling himself before God so that even as he was lifted up on a cross of abject sin, he submitted himself to the work of God birthing a new creation. By God's resurrection power at work even in death, Christ ransomed our captivity to sin and fear and hopelessness so that we, too, could stand like Christ for God and against the forces of evil to proclaim, "Enough! By God, enough!"

So we're here to praise God-power, to give thanks, to ask forgiveness for allowing sin to cause us to stumble, to exalt Jesus Christ as Lord of all. We're here to worship God as God through the Way, Jesus Christ. And as we submit our lives to God here, we practice how to live out our faith in the world. Opening ourselves further to God's resurrection power so our servant work in the world can glorify Christ, we become vessels of the Spirit, participating in the ongoing work of God struggling to birth the New Creation for all people. Lowering ourselves to be subject to Christ with all we are in all we do, we're taken up by the power of God's great reversal. As we humble ourselves to enthrone Christ, we're lifted up, exalted into the very heart of God.

So come on! Let's stand to exalt Jesus Christ as Lord of our lives, our church, and the whole world. Let's confess our faith with the simple words: Jesus Christ is Lord! Ready? Shout it out: Jesus Christ is Lord! (Move into a rousing hymn.)

SUGGESTIONS FOR WORSHIP

Call to Worship (from Psalms 47 and 93)

LEADER: Clap your hands, all ye people; Shout unto God with triumph:

PEOPLE: The Holy One is clothed with majesty, girded with strength. Our God rules!

LEADER: The Creator establishes divine rule from everlasting to everlasting.

PEOPLE: God goes up with the sound of the trumpet. Rejoice!

LEADER: Sing praises; sing praises to the Ruler of the whole earth,

PEOPLE: Sing praises, sing praises to God; sing praises!

Prayer of Confession

Exalted Christ, we stand amazed when we consider your glory. But you demand that we worship you through service to others, as well as in songs of praise. We confess that too often we come to worship to rest in your glory, to be recharged to live selfish lives. Concerned with getting and spending, we lay waste your powers. We care little about others far away and out of sight. We'd rather stay here to worship you. Forgive us, O Lord. Renew us with Holy Spirit, so we may be the body of Christ broken for the world, with an offering of praise in service to others. We ask all to your glory through Christ Jesus our Lord. Amen.

Assurance of Pardon

The same Christ who reigns in glory died for us that we might be made new. Trusting in the grace of God, go now to live Kingdom lives

125

as new creations in the discipline, freedom, and dominion of Jesus Christ. Amen.

Benediction (based on Ephesians 1:17)

May the God of our Lord Jesus Christ give you the Spirit of wisdom as you go out to live lives that glorify the Holy One, high and lifted up for our sakes, that we might be taken up into the Spirit of God.

To Christ be all power and glory and dominion now and forevermore! Amen.

1. This is said in such a way as to parody the movie *Titanic*. A word here about the traditional male language. Some will be uncomfortable with the use of *king, kingdom, Lord*. Though I used other terms as well, I used more traditional language than usual in order to get people on board with what I am talking about quickly. Consider these issues in your context.

2. From William Wordsworth, "Sonnet" ("The world is too much with us . . .").

Day of Pentecost

Dawn Darwin Weaks

Acts 2:1-21: The disciples' witness to the world begins with the coming of the Holy Spirit as Jesus promised.

Genesis 11:1-9: The storyteller answers our question of "Why so many languages?" in a way that exposes humanity's prideful, futile attempts to secure our own future.

Psalm 104:24-34, 35*b:* The psalmist shouts praise to God the Creator upon whose spirit all creation depends for life and growth.

Romans 8:14-17: Paul points the people to a new identity in Christ through the gift of the Spirit: We are children of God, co-heirs with Christ.

John 14:8-17 (25-27): Jesus tells the disciples that they are to continue his work with the guidance of the Holy Spirit, whom the Father will send.

REFLECTIONS

Jesus promised this would happen. The disciples were dutifully waiting together in Jerusalem, just as Jesus had instructed them. He had told them they would receive power from the Holy Spirit, a power that would send them out to begin their mission to the world. Sure enough, the Spirit came.

I don't know about your churches, but in my church we speak very tentatively of the Holy Spirit. We don't know how to talk about the Spirit or what the Spirit does exactly. For me, the Pentecost story is so striking because the signs of the Spirit's presence are vividly clear: wind, and fire, and the complete removal of any barriers to the

127

proclamation of the gospel of Jesus Christ. The Spirit came upon all of the disciples sitting in that house, and the gospel was heard by all of those in the crowds nearby. Perhaps most telling, the house the disciples were gathered in disappears from the story. The physical walls that separated them from the world in need of their witness have come down. They are suddenly standing in a crowd of thousands, even eventually standing in the waters of baptism with new converts to Christ. When our barriers to proclaiming the gospel are coming down, we can unabashedly say, "The Holy Spirit has come upon us!"

A SERMON BRIEF

If These Walls Could Talk

We don't talk about the Holy Spirit very often. When we start saying much about the Spirit, it's not long before our words get terribly vague. It's hard. But then, most of the really important, undeniably real things in life are hard to talk about.

"Talk about fire." We sat around the fire pit after a lovely day of camping. It was good to be warmed by the fire. The glowing embers turned from a bright yellow, to iridescent red as the evening waned.

No, you're talking about warmth, embers, not fire.

"Describe wind." Sitting on the porch swing in the evening. Amazingly warm for this early in June. A rustle in the leaves, growing stronger. The wind chimes make music. I am refreshed.

No. That's leaves in trees, metal knocking against metal. Talk about *wind*.

Now describe the Holy Spirit.

Well, it—wait, there's the first problem. "It"—the Holy Spirit is not an "it." The Holy Spirit is a person. But Spirit doesn't have gender, so we run into a language problem right away.

Let me just tell you what happened on the birthing day of the church. The disciples were gathered together in a house, waiting for the Spirit to come as Jesus had promised. Sure enough, She-He—the Holy Spirit—came upon them that day, like wind, like fire. Ken Medema sings this song: "I think I see some sunlight, comin' through a crack in the wall ... and I'm gonna sing this song 'til the walls start a-tumblin' down."[1]

Well, the walls tumbled down that day. The walls that separated who could preach the gospel and who could not came down. The prophet Joel's vision was fulfilled—*all* flesh was blessed by the Holy Spirit to proclaim the gospel. Not just the male and the educated, but male and female, old and young, slave and free—they all became ministers of the gospel of Jesus Christ. And the walls that separated who could hear the gospel and who could not came down. The walls separating people from this country and from that country, the walls separating my language from your language, the walls separating the generations of young and old, the walls separating the haves and the have-nots—they all came a-tumblin' down! The gospel was proclaimed for the first time across barriers of nationality and language. And the people understood and were saved.

Maybe you missed it, but one more set of walls came down when the Spirit came upon them that day. Notice this passage started out with the disciples safely in a house. But somehow and somewhere in the story, the Spirit brought down even the physical walls that separated the disciples from the world around them. Suddenly, they are outside proclaiming the gospel to thousands of people. Later that day, they are gathered around a body of water, baptizing people left and right.

That's the Holy Spirit. We know some things only by their effects. Breaking down walls is an unmistakable sign of the Spirit at work: As the sound of leaves rustling lets you know the wind is there, as the smell of smoke lets you know there's fire, an ever-expanding circle of believers lets you know the Spirit is there.

So, is the Spirit here, in the church today? Do we see the Spirit's effects?

Sunday morning at 11 o'clock is still the most segregated hour in the United States. But in our church, we are blessed by brave African Americans, Native Americans, Asian Americans, and Hispanic Americans who are willing to worship with a bunch of white folk. I think I see some sunlight comin' through a crack in the wall. . . .

The world's largest Protestant denomination still proclaims that women cannot be pastors. But in our church just last week, I saw a little girl tiptoe up to the pulpit and pretend to preach to the imaginary people in the pews. I think I see some sunlight. . . .

Our society has categorized us by age: the boomers, the Xers, the World War II generations, and the church often mirrors that separation. But in our church, two of our strongest leaders are working together on a project—Leonard is 80; Pennie is 30. I think I see some sunlight. . . .

There's no doubt in my mind, there's no hesitation in my speech—the Holy Spirit is upon us! We who are gathered together in this place have been touched by the flames of fire and swept up into the winds of change. Old and young, male and female, black, white, red, yellow, and brown—we all have heard the gospel and we all have been empowered by the Spirit to go and share it. Now, look out! We think it's just us gathered here in this house. But look again—we find ourselves surrounded by three thousand of our neighbors who want to hear about Jesus. They have heard the Spirit speaking their language. Will the Spirit move us beyond these walls? Sure as the sound of rustling leaves lets you know the wind is there, sure as the smell of smoke lets you know there's fire, an ever-expanding circle of believers lets you know the Spirit is here. And the Spirit is about to take us out there! The walls are a-tumblin', the walls are a-tumblin' down!

SUGGESTIONS FOR WORSHIP

Call to Worship (based on Psalm 104:24-34)

LEADER: O Lord, all of your many works sing your praises!
PEOPLE: **You create the world in beauty; you sustain all of creation with your goodness.**
LEADER: You send your Spirit, and we are renewed.
PEOPLE: **May our worship be pleasing as we rejoice in you!**

Prayer of Confession and Assurance of Pardon (based on John 14:8-17, 25-27)

Powerful God, you have sent your Son to be our Savior and your Spirit to be our Sustainer. Yet we continue to resist your call to be witnesses of your love to those around us. We insist on spending our energies erecting barriers you have already removed. Forgive us when our need to remain comfortable keeps us from courageously sharing the good news. Renew us by your mercy and send us out again to be your servants. Amen.

LEADER: Children of God, hear the word of the Lord: "Do not let your hearts be troubled. Trust in God. I will do whatever you ask in my name." You have been restored. Even now the Spirit fills you again.

Benediction

Do you sense the wind and fire in your bones? The Holy Spirit is upon you, empowering you to share the gospel of Jesus Christ. You cannot stay here! Go, and tell the good news! Amen.

1. Ken Medema, "Crack in the Wall" (Grandville, Mich.: Brier Patch Music, 1992).

Ordinary Time 11 or Proper 6

Dusty Kenyon Fiedler

1 Kings 21:1-10 (11-14), 15-21*a:* In this familiar story of Naboth's vineyard, Queen Jezebel plots to get the land illegally for her husband King Ahab, but the Lord's prophet Elijah promises disaster for Ahab.

Psalm 5:1-8: The psalmist prays for God's protection and a clear sense of God's call and responds to God's faithfulness with reverent worship.

Galatians 2:15-21: Paul argues that we are "justified" by God's great grace in Christ Jesus, not by the old duties of the Law. All who want to follow—Jews and even Gentiles—live in faith and live for God.

Luke 7:36–8:3: When a Pharisee named Simon invites Jesus home for dinner, they are both surprised by the presence of a "sinful" woman who wipes Jesus' feet with her tears and then pours costly perfume on them. Jesus tells Simon a story about two men who owed debts they could not pay, and then Jesus explains the woman's great act of love. The text ends with a report about women who are also following Jesus (and helping to pay for his needs).

REFLECTIONS

The Gospel lesson is a wonderful text for a Communion or stewardship sermon. (The Eleventh Sunday in Ordinary Time occurs too early for the usual fall stewardship campaign, but it offers a chance to raise stewardship themes at another time of year.) I suggest this because of the story's context: It takes place at the table, and it shows us how abundantly God gives (and forgives).

Luke reports that Jesus "went into the Pharisee's house and took his place at the table," but after this, *nothing* in the story seems "in place." The woman of the street enters from nowhere (How does she gain entry/access to this special guest?), and the Pharisee sees his world of safe assumptions turned upside down. Jesus shatters the status quo with another example of amazing grace at work as he tells a story to show how different God's way is from the usual way things are done.

One of the intriguing parts of this story of the "sinful" woman who bathes Jesus' feet is how Luke lets us listen in on the host Pharisee as he talks to himself: "If this man were a prophet, he would have known who and what kind of woman this is who is touching him— that she is a sinner." But all along Jesus knows this *and* what the Pharisee is thinking to himself! We see so clearly in this story how well Jesus knows us all. Here Christ tries to help the Pharisee see what generous love is all about. This woman loves so much, so generously, because she has been forgiven so much, Jesus says. The Pharisee, like many of us, is left to ponder his own stingy response to Jesus. And in contrast, the woman, this "sinner," goes in peace, with Christ's declaration ringing in her heart: "Your faith has saved you."

A SERMON BRIEF

I knew he was a special child long before I met him. It was his school bus that was my clue: yellow and standard, like all the rest, but much shorter—a "special" bus—and I had watched him run down the steps and into the woman's waiting arms day after day. He was about six, I guessed, and even from across the meadow I could tell he was a bundle of energy. And so much more! I can't even remember how we actually met, but once I got to know Seth, he was in my heart forever. He was a child with Down's Syndrome, but that label hardly described all in him that was funny and cheerful and clever and happy. And loving—oh, so *full* of love. His mother claimed that he did have a few tears or pouts on occasion, but I never saw Seth without the biggest smile on his face and his arms outstretched for hug— both to give and to get. I always hoped I would see Seth on the days that *I* was pouting or sad (more often than I'd like to admit), because it was impossible to stay blue or angry in Seth's exuberant presence. And the word "unselfish" was made for him. Seth was always giving things to others—his lunch, his beloved gumdrops (usually sticky—

but still precious!), special rocks he had found on the road, hugs and hugs and more hugs. When Seth walked into a room, it was like sunshine itself warming everyone. I often thought how different (and better) our world would be if we were all like Seth. It was as if he did not know how *not* to love.

I think Jesus wants us to see that God is like that—only greater. In God's view, Seth's loving nature is what is "normal"—loving with abandon, with no caution or calculation. It's all about thinking of the other. It's how the woman from the city loves Jesus: with her tears, her kisses, her costly ointment. Though she seems to appear out of nowhere, somehow this woman knows even before he says the words that Jesus forgives her. And her response to his gracious mercy knows no bounds.

On the other hand, the righteous Pharisee seems very uncomfortable with her presence and her behavior. Something—pride? fear? an inability to believe that God could love him so much?—something strong and sinister prevents his responding to Jesus so gratefully. She whom he labels the "sinner" gives a generous and grateful response to Christ's love and forgiveness, but he, the "noble" churchman, stingily holds back. He (grudgingly, it seems) concedes that those who have experienced the greatest cancellation of their sin will love the most—but he seems unable to accept his own need for forgiveness. He stays stuck.

Ah, it's so easy to poke fun now at those Pharisees of long ago. They allow us to feel pretty good about our own response, until we ask ourselves seriously: Am I ready to love Jesus wholeheartedly, without counting the cost, like this "sinful" woman? I asked our seventh-grade Confirmation Class about this Gospel story: "Which of these two people is more like you?" Too many answered, "The Pharisee, because it's hard not to be selfish." One said, honestly and thoughtfully, "I like to think I love Jesus like that woman—so joyfully and unselfishly. But don't ask me about loving real people like that. Then for sure I'm the selfish, in-control Pharisee."

Ah—there's the rub! Getting down to practical, real people. Why is it that we think so much? For dear Seth, there *is* nothing but the real thing, and loving seems so natural. It gives so much joy—for him, I think, but certainly I know how much joy his loving gives to others. Jesus seems so clear: "I know all about you—and still I love you. I love you more than you can ever imagine! Why can't you understand that? You make simple things so hard and complicated. Now go, and love likewise. You'll make my day—and your own!"

June 13, 2004

SUGGESTIONS FOR WORSHIP

Call to Worship

LEADER: Jesus calls to us: Come, join me at the table. Let us all take our places.

PEOPLE: **Where shall we sit, Lord? Is there room enough for all? Do I belong here?**

LEADER: With Christ there is *always* enough—enough room, enough bread, enough love and forgiveness.

PEOPLE: **O Lord, we accept your invitation—for we see that it is you who will make us worthy. We come with joy! We come to love you, for we see how much you love us!**

ALL: **We come to Christ's table as Christ's precious guests. ALLELUIA!**

Prayer of Confession

Gracious God: Forgive us when we act like self-righteous people who do not need your help or your forgiveness. We can be so stingy with our love. We hold back loving you, our families, our neighbors, even ourselves. Change our hearts, O God, and remake us according to the example of Jesus Christ, in whom we pray. Amen.

Assurance of Pardon

LEADER: This is good news, friends: Christ says to each one of us: "Your sins are forgiven."

PEOPLE: **He wants us to accept this great gift—and we do! Thanks be to God!**

LEADER: Now go in peace, as forgiven people who have been made whole in Christ Jesus.

Benediction

May courage, joy, an abiding hope, and all the good gifts of our Lord Jesus Christ be yours, and may you go in peace. Amen.

135

Ordinary Time 13 or Proper 8

Sandra Sonhyang Kim

---

2 Kings 2:1-2, 6-14: Elijah casts his mantle upon Elisha and then ascends into heaven.

Psalm 77:1-2, 11-20: The psalmist, in distress, cries out to God and is comforted through a recounting of God's "wonders of old."

Galatians 5:1, 13-25: Paul calls Christians to a responsible demonstration of their freedom in Christ.

Luke 9:51-62: A Samaritan village rejects Jesus' disciples, prompting Jesus to reiterate the demands of following him.

REFLECTIONS

The Rev. Son Yang Won lost both his sons during the Communist Revolution in 1947 in Yosu, Korea. During the funeral of his sons he shared the following tearful list of thanksgivings: I thank God for allowing a wretched sinner like me to have two sons who were martyred for God's glory; I thank God for allowing me to sacrifice the first born and the second born sons to God (he had two sons and a daughter); I thank God for allowing my sons to preach the gospel until the time of their deaths; I thank God for allowing my two sons to be in a better kingdom than the United States of America where they were preparing to travel to pursue further education. The list goes on. But there is one thanksgiving that always gets the attention of those who hear this story: "I thank God for allowing me to love the enemy who killed my two sons."

History testifies that not only did the Rev. Son pray for Jae-sun An, who was waiting to be prosecuted for the killing of Son's two sons, but he pleaded with government officials to set An free. The Rev. Son changed Jae-sun An to Jae-sun Son, adopting the released culprit as his own one and only son. After the adoption, Jae-sun, as the son of the Rev. Son, pursued a theological education and became a pastor himself.

As we encounter stories of amazing love such as this, we wonder how it is possible. Paul, in Galatians 5, answers that it is through the guidance of the Spirit that Christ-bearers are able to love one another. He further points out that love comes from the freedom given in Christ who demonstrated amazing love with his own life.

This sermon is modified from a message shared with entering college students of the Richmond Korean Central Presbyterian Church in Virginia.

A SERMON BRIEF

Last week I enjoyed spending time with some of you who are entering college this year. I'm sure you are a bit scared as well as very excited about the new life you are soon to begin. If any of you are like me, you have been ready to leave home for some time now. In a few days your struggle to meet curfews, your restricted driving privileges, those constant interruptions from siblings, and your parents' efforts to share their "wisdom for your well-being" will be things of the past— well, maybe not the last one, but it will be nicely recorded on your answering machine for you to listen to when you are "available"!

When you get to your dorm room, there will be your new best friend named "freedom," waiting for you with open arms. Being free is one of the deepest human desires. It's a desire held not only by those of you who are leaving home for the first time but by all of us who feel bound by life's various restrictions. However, as you shout, "Free at last!" I invite you to take some time to reflect on this freedom. You may realize that freedom creates more than bubbles of excitement. It also generates a somewhat uncomfortable feeling deep down in your heart and requires at least some sort of new rules—perhaps even a totally new pattern of life.

I remember vividly what I did with my newly granted freedom during the first year of college. I had set up a place for study at the beach, but whenever the sun came out I studied nature instead of my assignments! "I'll study and catch up on rainy days," I reasoned. What happened? Well, there just weren't enough rainy days, and I had to make up my work the hard way.

The theme of what to do with freedom is not at all unique to college freshmen. Christians in Galatia had a very similar problem with their newly given freedom. What is at stake for the Galatians? Are some of them entering colleges for the first time and moving into the newly built Galatia University dorms? Well, not exactly.

Paul had left Galatia after preaching that Christians are free because Christ has freed them; they no longer were slaves to the law. As a result, some Galatians were marveling at the idea of living a lawless life. However, these wondering Galatians became more perplexed when some teachers came along and instructed the new Christians that Paul was completely wrong. They argued that Paul's message of Christ was not enough to obtain salvation. What the Galatians really needed was circumcision in order to be certain of their justification. So some of them began to question whether or not to cut off a part of their flesh. "Ouch!" you might exclaim.

But Paul sent a different message in his letter. "Just say no!" he beseeches the Galatians after he received news of what was going on. With this 1980s anti-drug slogan, Paul goes on to remind the Galatians of the freedom they had gained in Christ and urges them not to go back to the slavery of the law. If the Galatians submitted to circumcision according to the law, then they would be responsible for obeying all the other laws as well. Furthermore, Paul teaches that the function of the law is to guard minors; for fully grown adults it would be sheer foolishness to submit to their childhood guardian and be once again cut off from the freedom that has been granted to them.

Then what are we to do with our freedom? the Galatians asked. Paul replies that rather than using freedom to return to the law, they are to exercise their freedom to *love*. "You shall love your neighbor as yourself." With this summation of the whole law, Paul reminds them that love is the fulfillment of all the law. Further, Paul urges that this love should not be self-indulgent since love ultimately comes from Jesus Christ who denied himself and gave up his own life for all. Because of Christ's sacrifice, we have the privilege of extravagantly spending our freedom on love, joy, peace, patience, kindness, generosity, faithfulness, gentleness, and self-control. These are not just nice thoughts but decisive acts that issue from Christ's self-giving. In his freedom he chose to love us, and by his love we are now living in freedom. Rather than going back to become slaves to the law, the Galatian Christians were called to follow the footsteps of Jesus to become slaves to one another and servants of love to edify the whole community of believers.

What about us? What do you think we are called to do? Paul tells us that we live in the Spirit of God that enables us to enjoy what Christ has provided for us: all the fruit of the Spirit, all the benefits of his love.

So what will you do with your new life of freedom in Christ? Since we are freed from many of the rules that have guided and protected us so far, should we continue to observe them? Perhaps. But more important than meeting the arbitrary curfew and driving restrictions is living as responsible and compassionate people who belong to Christ Jesus. With thanksgiving, let us be guided by the Spirit into a life of love.

SUGGESTIONS FOR WORSHIP

Call to Worship (adapted from Psalm 77:11-15)

LEADER: We remember the wonderful deeds of your great love, O God.

PEOPLE: **We meditate on all your works and praise your everlasting love.**

LEADER: Your way, O God, is holy. What god is so great as our God?

PEOPLE: **We remember the mighty deeds you have done.**

LEADER: We recall the strong arms of love that freed your people.

PEOPLE: **As God's loved and freed people, let us worship our God together.**

Prayer of Confession

LEADER: Eternal God, through the death of Jesus Christ you freed us long ago, yet we come before you this day feeling bound by old sins and desires.

PEOPLE: **Forgive us, O Lord.**

LEADER: Through the love shown in the life of Jesus Christ you have always loved us, yet we come before you this day wondering whether we are loved.

PEOPLE: **Forgive us, O Lord.**

LEADER: Through the wisdom of your Spirit you have always guided us, yet we come before you this day wondering if we can find our way.

PEOPLE: **Forgive us, O Lord. Remake us once again this day to live as your freed, loved, and guided people who are faithful to the call to love others.**

Assurance of Pardon

It is through Christ Jesus who was crucified that we are forgiven. Those who belong to Christ have crucified the flesh with its passions and desires. Live and be guided by the Spirit and know that we are not only forgiven but also strengthened to be ambassadors of love.

Benediction

As we leave this place as the freed and loved people of Jesus Christ, may the freedom of Christ, the love of God, and the guidance of the Spirit go with you. And let us be the instruments Christ's everlasting love by embracing sisters and brothers of all nations and people near and far.

Ordinary Time 25 or Proper 20

Kerra Becker English

> **Jeremiah 8:18–9:1:** Jeremiah mourns for the people who cry, "The harvest is past, the summer is ended, and we are not saved."
>
> **Psalm 79:1-9:** The psalmist pleas for God's mercy upon Jerusalem, which lies in ruins.
>
> **1 Timothy 2:1-7:** Paul encourages Timothy to pray that all will come to the knowledge of the truth of God in Jesus Christ.
>
> **Luke 16:1-13:** The parable of the dishonest manager.

REFLECTIONS

A challenge in preaching from the prophets is to bring the prophetic message into today's context without alienating one's listeners—the never-ending struggle between being prophetic and being pastoral. This passage from Jeremiah that is included in the "oracles of judgment" offers a harsh critique of the religious community's capitulation to powerful forces within the culture. It builds on a prosaic sermon against temple worship that precedes it in chapter 7. But in Jeremiah, we meet both the prophet who pronounces God's judgment and the pastor who weeps as a spiritual winter destroys that which is not strong enough or faithful enough to survive.

Biblical time frequently alludes to spiritual seasons that allegorically correspond to our annual seasons, and for some in-depth understanding of how one might interpret history in such a fashion, I would recommend reading *The Fourth Turning* by historians William Strauss and Neil Howe. Although the book is written as an analysis of the turning points in U.S. history, one can infer that there are repeated patterns in history's cleansing ritual of death and rebirth (a resurrection theme no less!).

What I hope to convey in every sermon I preach is a sense that God is, God was, and God will be in the future, whether we happen to be there or not. It helps me in times of chaos and crisis, whether personal, congregational, national, or global, to adjust my all-too-human focus and try to become more *theocentric*. In times of great distress, a "me-only" or "just us" attitude will be doomed to failure. Prophetic pastors will resonate with Jeremiah's need to call attention to the longer history in which God is always faithful, even if we cannot always sense that faithfulness in our own little slice of time.

A SERMON BRIEF

Jeremiah was the proverbial preacher's kid. He grew up in the shadow of the Jerusalem Temple. He felt the omnipresence of God in the ever-watchful eyes of the priests and in the even more scrutinizing eyes of the congregants. At home, he probably heard conversations with regularity about the ups and downs of this profession. His own family had been involved in one of the most notorious splits the Temple had ever known. Because of King Solomon's jealousy over political loyalties, Jeremiah's ancestor Abiathar had been banished from the temple priesthood where he formerly shared the title of "Chief Priest" with only one other person. From an early age, Jeremiah learned about the treacherous intermingling of religion and politics, a lesson he would find himself reliving in his life as a prophet.

Yes, Jeremiah knew that in the very heart of religious life there is a dangerous place where faithfulness and faithlessness collide. He felt in his gut the intensity of his own family story that involved betrayal from the community of faith they held so dear. His family loved God, but sometimes hated God's people. When Abiathar stood against the pretentiousness of the Davidic monarchy, his family ended up betrayed by those the community held in high regard. Many nights, perhaps, Jeremiah heard from his own bed the sobs of his loved ones as they cried out to God for justice, as they wept for a people turned away from God by unscrupulous priests seeking personal power. Jeremiah's own eyes grew red with the tears of those who care.

Growing up in this environment, teased and tormented, Jeremiah had no choice but to develop a tough skin. God used Jeremiah's suffering to polish his passion as an oyster polishes the irritating grain of sand into a beautiful pearl. God also had had enough of the faithlessness of this people. The Temple that was supposed to be a place of peace had become a palace for the powerful here on earth. No longer were the orphans, widows, and foreigners shown the hospitality of God's love. No longer were the warnings against stealing, murder, and adultery heeded. No longer did God have primary place in the people's worship or in their lives. The life of faith was being mocked from all angles, from every corner, everywhere. Someone had to be sent to them with the message of God's tough love. Jeremiah was in the right place at the right time to bring God's own message of righteous indignation.

And still today, too often *faith* has less to do with how we live our lives and more to do with a particular "name-brand" of religion. Faith is a preference, something we check off on a form rather than that which precipitates the most meaningful decisions of our lives. When asked about our faith, we casually say, "I'm Presbyterian (or Methodist, or Baptist), what are you?"

That isn't all it's supposed to be! Jeremiah knew that, and we need the reminder ourselves. In Jeremiah's day, religious affiliation with the Temple had become suspect. The institution specifically charged with keeping God's mandates here on earth had broken its promises to those it was called to serve. Jeremiah pleaded with the people of God to break ranks with this earthly authority and instead be subject to the divine will.

In nearly every lifetime, there comes a point at which we must reckon with Jeremiah's ghost. If we let him, Jeremiah reminds us of how much richer our religious life can be when we put our trust fully in God. He pushes the radical belief that it's more important to be faithful to God than it is to be faithful to any organization that claims to have true knowledge of God. So in order for us to honor the message God spoke so urgently through Jeremiah, we must ask ourselves: Does my faith community put its trust in God or only in the appearance of worshiping God?

During the lives of all religious communities, we have the peculiar need for the cleansing purgation of bleak spiritual winters that allow us to feel the deadness of the structures we have built unto ourselves, and make room for the coming spring that renews and rejuvenates our faith in God alone. Jeremiah and God mourn together the recurrence of this Passover angel that will leave death in its wake:

My joy is gone, grief is upon me,
    my heart is sick.
Hark, the cry of my poor people
    from far and wide in the land:
"Is the LORD not in Zion?
    Is her King not in her?"
("Why have they provoked me to anger with their images,
    with their foreign idols?")
"The harvest is past, the summer is ended,
    and we are not saved." (Jeremiah 8:18-20)

God weeps for the people as destructive forces are unleashed from every corner to wreak havoc on the land, the nation, and, at its very core, the center of worship in Jerusalem. Jeremiah weeps alongside God as though his "head were a spring of water." So when he asks the rhetorical questions, "Is there no balm in Gilead? Is there no physician there?" Jeremiah already knows that nothing will ease this pain. There will be no comfort, no healing, no salvation that can soothe what's about to take place. Our religious symbols remind us that pain and death must precede healing and hope. The flood before the rainbow, the wilderness before the promised land, the cross before the empty tomb, the sting of repentance before the salve of forgiveness.

When our religious communities are quick to offer easy solutions that please the masses instead of offering the deep wrestling that it takes to be faithful to God's calling, they have failed to recognize the spiritual winter. That's when Jeremiah's ghost will reappear bringing the painful, tearful message that God is heartsick at our lack of faith. Jeremiah's family history taught him to be cautiously aware that faith in God and faith in the church are not the same thing. God alone is worthy of our worship. And in God's time, in God's turning of the seasons, the promised hope is that spring will come, and with it the tears we shed over winter will become the balm that heals us.

SUGGESTIONS FOR WORSHIP

Call to Worship

(a dialogue between the "weeping prophet" and Psalm 79)

LEADER: Is there a balm in Gilead?

PEOPLE: **O God, the nations have come into your inheritance, but have defiled your holy Temple.**

LEADER: Is there no physician there?

PEOPLE: **They have laid Jerusalem in ruins.**

LEADER: When will the wounded receive healing?

PEOPLE: **They have given the bodies of your servants to the birds of the air for food, the flesh of your faithful to the wild animals of the earth.**

LEADER: When will the weary find salvation?

PEOPLE: **Our blood is poured out like water. No one will bury our dead.**

LEADER: How long, O Lord? Will you be angry forever?

PEOPLE: **Help us, O God of our salvation, for the glory of your name; deliver us, and forgive our sins, for your name's sake!**

Benediction

Take courage, and do not fear. For everything there is a season, and a time for every purpose under heaven. Go in peace knowing that in whatever time or season you find yourself, God is faithful still. Amen.

All Saints Day

Ruthanna B. Hooke

Daniel 7:1-3, 15-18: Daniel's vision of the four winds and the four beasts is reported and interpreted, with the assurance that God's holy ones shall "possess the kingdom forever."

Psalm 149: This psalm invites dancing and singing in praise of God and invokes punishment upon the enemies of God's people.

Ephesians 1:11-23: In Christ, believers have received a "glorious inheritance" of God's power working for them.

Luke 6:20-31: Jesus invokes blessings and woes upon the people.

REFLECTIONS

In this sermon, I draw on the readings from Ephesians and Luke to reflect on the doctrine of the communion of saints. In Ephesians the term *saints* refers to the entire membership of the Christian community. More recently, the term has come to refer to Christians of particular holiness, and especially to those who have died. In my denomination, Episcopalian, the Feast of All Saints and the following day, All Souls Day, are days set aside to remember all the faithful departed, especially those "ordinary saints," who do not have a feast day of their own. At the same time, this feast is a day in which we remember our intercommunion with all the faithful, the living and the dead, and in fellowship with them we recommit ourselves to Christian discipleship. I try to combine these emphases in this sermon.

Underlying the sermon is a rather Roman Catholic theology of the saints, in which the saints who have died are not just a memory but an active presence in our lives, who assist us in our own efforts to be faithful disciples of Jesus Christ. The sermon is interactive; at one point I invite all in the congregation to come up, name someone who was a saint for them, and light a candle in their honor. I do this because I want to create a visual representation (a church full of lit candles) of the belief I am proclaiming, namely that the saints surround us always and shine their light upon us. The litany included under "Suggestions for Worship" is also an effort to create the sense of the great cloud of witnesses surrounding and empowering us. In thus upholding us, the saints give us the courage to be saints ourselves, faithful to the promised inheritance of God's realm of justice and peace.

A SERMON BRIEF

To Be in That Number

Delight Kirtland. Richard Dickinson. Thomas Page. Do you know these people? They are with us every Sunday. Their names are in our stained glass windows, on cushions and chalices. Mary Ives's name is carved into the font. The altar candlesticks were given in memory of Samuel Stewart. The cross on the altar has William Cook's name on it. When you start looking around, the names are everywhere, reminding us that there are many more people worshiping with us here than we can see.

Today is All Saints Day, when we remember and celebrate our ancestors in the faith. In Ephesians they are those who have been sealed by the Holy Spirit and promised a glorious inheritance from God. Jesus, in Luke's Gospel, calls them the blessed ones, who loved their enemies, who endured persecution for the sake of God's realm. We remember the famous saints of ages past, like Bridget, an abbess who founded monasteries in Ireland. Or Francis, renowned for his generosity to the poor. Or Oscar Romero, murdered for his work with the oppressed in El Salvador. But on All Saints Day we particularly remember the more ordinary saints, people who were not famous and yet were faithful, who strove to love their enemies, to be generous without thought of reward, who lived in hope of inheriting God's promised realm. Such are the folk whose names are written around this church—on our windows, candlesticks, fonts and crosses. Today is a day to honor them.

Perhaps you can think of someone who has died who is a saint for

147

you. It could be anyone you have known who modeled what it means to trust in God's promises and hope for God's realm. Someone whom you hold in your heart, whom you remember today. I invite you to come forward, say their names, and then light a candle and bring it back to your seat. [Pause while people do this]

What have we just created? I said at the outset that today we *remember* the saints. But we are not only remembering them, as though they were a past reality. The saints are not just a memory; they are a living presence. All the people you have named, all those whose names are found throughout this church, and all the faithful of every generation are with us each day. When we light these candles, we only make visible the light that they shine in our world. Our belief in the resurrection of the dead tells us that those who have died do not just *stop*, but they continue. They continue to be with us, and to be active.

Their active presence in our lives gives us a call and a gift. The call is simply to follow where they have led the way. "Since we are surrounded by so great a cloud of witnesses, . . . let us run with perseverance the race that is set before us," says the letter to the Hebrews [12:1]. We are accountable to our ancestors in the faith, to continue the great work they have begun. Francis urges me to give generously to those in need, Bridget calls me to be powerful in God's service, and Oscar Romero prompts me to hunger for righteousness. Lucy, Richard, and all the others memorialized here call us to support this community of faith, which they loved. The people for whom you hold candles inspire you to carry on the best of who they were and what they did.

The *gift* the saints give us is to help us carry out this call. Our belief in the *communion* of saints tells us that we are connected with the faithful of all times and places, from Francis to Oscar Romero to Mary Ives. We are connected in one Body under Christ our head, and the power Christ gave to them is also given to us. When we seek to follow in their footsteps, to hunger for righteousness or to love our enemies, we draw strength from the saints who have gone before us. They give us the stamina to persevere just when we feel our own strength is gone.

The gift the saints give us is not only strength in God's service, but also a vision of the goal toward which we strive. The saints even now stand in God's presence, bathed in God's love and beholding God's glory, beholding the fulfillment of God's realm of justice and peace, which exists in heaven as one day it will on earth. Because we are connected with them, we share, even in this life, a glimpse of their vision, their glorious inheritance. Every Sunday during the Eucharist we claim to join with all the company of heaven as we sing "Holy, holy, holy," to join for a moment the song being sung in heaven. When we take Communion we get a taste of the banquet that the saints enjoy in heaven. We dare to believe that, even as we now commune with them in Spirit, we will one day be joined to them in the bliss of heaven. We dare to hope that, as the song says, we will be in that number when the saints go marching in. We dare to trust that we will see with them the fulfillment of God's realm of justice and peace. We dare to pray that at the last day we will feast together in the presence of the one who is the source of the saints' courage and joy, Jesus Christ himself.

When you come to the altar rail to receive the foretaste of that banquet, imagine that all the saints are with you, as they will be on that last day. Imagine that away to your left, stretching off to infinity, all the saints who have ever lived are standing at the rail. And away to the right, imagine all the saints yet to come, standing at the rail. Feel your connection to them all. Let their vision of heaven recommit you to the work of love and righteousness they have begun here on earth. Nourish your hope that one day we will all be in that number, when the saints go marching in.

SUGGESTIONS FOR WORSHIP

Call to Worship

LEADER: O God, you have surrounded us with a cloud of witness too great to number.

ALL: **You have made us one body with all your faithful ones.**

LEADER: Open our eyes to see their vision.

ALL: **Fill us with their courage and joy.**

Litany of the Saints

LEADER: Mary Magdalene, witness to the resurrection

ALL: **Present with us now.**

LEADER: Paul, proclaimer of faith's foolishness

ALL: **Present with us now.**

LEADER:	Stephen, first martyr for Christ
ALL:	**Present with us now.**
LEADER:	Francis, joyful in poverty
ALL:	**Present with us now.**
LEADER:	Teresa, teacher of holiness
ALL:	**Present with us now.**
LEADER:	Bonhoeffer, fearless witness to justice
ALL:	**Present with us now.**
LEADER:	O God of all the saints, you are present with us now. In your strength all the saints found courage and joy in ages past. Kindle in us their same courage; help us to draw on their presence, that we might live as they did, faithful witnesses to your glory, fearless servants of your kingdom.
ALL:	**Amen.**

Benediction

May Jesus Christ, who is the strength of the saints on earth, and the bliss of the saints in heaven, empower you to follow in their footsteps, to be joyful and courageous in God's service. Amen.

Christ the King (or Reign of Christ) Sunday

Nancy Ellett Allison

Jeremiah 23:1-6: Jeremiah prophesies woe upon those who have led God's people astray and anticipates the coming of the "righteous Branch" of David.

Luke 1:68-79: Zechariah's prophecy echoes that of Jeremiah, anticipating the one who will "give light to those who sit in darkness and in the shadow of death."

Colossians 1:11-20: Paul declares the supremacy of Christ.

Luke 23:33-43: Jesus is crucified and derided as "King of the Jews."

REFLECTIONS

On this Reign of Christ Sunday as a holy year draws to an end, we find in Colossians a celebration of the supremacy of Christ over all Creation. For Luke, forgiveness and reconciliation will mark this reign. This is a Sunday to enlarge our vision of the Christ whose reign has come and is yet to be completed, to expand our understandings of a world where nothing exists apart from the redemptive work of Christ.

A SERMON BRIEF

The Image of the Invisible

Imagine stretching in bed and having this as your first thought: "I arise today through the strength of heaven: light of sun, brilliance of

151

moon, splendor of fire, speed of lightning, swiftness of wind, depth of sea, stability of earth, firmness of rock." This Celtic prayer, the Deer Cry, is attributed to St. Patrick. Sure, this is the way I begin each day! How about you? To be honest, most of us do not imagine the strength of heaven and the swiftness of wind being the energies that compel us forward in the day. Those who do bound out of bed with "the splendor of fire" are those who welcome the day as high adventure, which often means those not yet burdened by work or school or the responsibilities of home life.

Fred Craddock tells of childhood days when his family would "go marveling" in the woods and simply absorb the beauty around them. As we look at this extraordinary passage in Colossians, I want you to do something that will open the spaces of your mind and heart to the poetry of scripture as you "go marveling" with me.

Close your eyes, relax. Remember a time when you walked by a stream, the beach, sat on a porch, enjoyed a concert, held hands with someone and found an expansive place in your soul. Move into that place. . . .

Now listen to Paul who is more a mystic than a systematic theologian in Colossians. First he reminds the Colossians of his prayers and devotion (vv. 3-4), his hopes for their lives (vv. 9-12), and then he "goes marveling" as he sings them a love song of creation (vv. 15-20). In this ancient hymn, perhaps from the Jewish Wisdom tradition, Paul transfers the preeminence of Wisdom to the role of the reigning Christ.

For Paul, Christ is the uniting essence of the universe; in Christ all reality "coheres." Teilhard de Chardin gave new language to that concept through articulating a third nature of Christ, not human or divine, but cosmic, encompassing the unimaginable infinite, beyond human, beyond divine, Christ in all. Matthew Fox expands this concept in *The Coming of the Cosmic Christ*. He writes of an alive and vital Cosmic Christ who is "the 'pattern that connects' all the atoms and galaxies of the universe, a pattern of divine love and justice that all creatures and all humans bear within them."[1]

Quantum physicists are as likely to use this language as theologians. The scientific shift from a Newtonian, mechanistic worldview to an integrated, relational universe signals a change in our understanding of reality and an opportunity to recreate Christology. In quantum theory, every element of the universe is composed of subatomic particle-waves. These particles can be measured as "packets" or "quanta" to locate where they are; or they can be evaluated like sound or light waves to tell how fast they are moving. Interestingly, each interaction impacts the particle-wave and changes its reality. This power of communication causes the atoms of one entity to inter-mingle with the energy fields of another in a way that increases the internal relationship of the whole universe. In other words, while it may be infinitesimal, a surge in the "radiance of the moon" does have an effect upon our lives, as does our early morning prayer have an impact on the "strength of heaven." These subatomic particle waves, the building blocks of our universe, are no more controllable than the waves of the ocean. They are constantly expanding and replenishing. While we see matter, a pulpit for example, as something isolated and discrete, it is better imagined as connected and condensed energy—energy that is profoundly social, waiting to interact with its environ-ment. Its energy, its entire structure, can be changed and released with a match.

In like manner, our interior lives are connected with every opera-tion of the universe. When we go marveling in this great world, as our soul is nourished by the grains of sand on the beach and by the sun on our arms, so too are the grains and the waves and the fish within them nourished by our presence. We know when we have entered a holy environment; we can feel the spirit, the energy of the place permeating our bones. The psalmist notes that "deep calls to deep" (Psalm 42:7).

And Paul asserts in Colossians that it is the Cosmic Christ who con-nects us to all things and to all people of all times. Remember John Donne's "No man is an island." The preexistent Christ, the image of the invisible God, who is before all things and in whom all things hold together, the head of created order and the head of the church, the incarnate Christ made real in Jesus, is the one who brings all things into reconciliation with God. Before all time Christ is; as time ends, Christ is. Wherever we go, from field to forest, from work to home, from heights to depths, we can find a reflection of God in Christ as we intentionally relate to the world around us. But we must open our eyes, we must "go marveling" for such grace to happen. We must know the Cosmic Christ who is the image of the invisible God, and we must search for this One in all people, all places, and all expe-riences of life.

The abbot of a well-known monastery went deep into the desert seeking guidance from a hermit. The once-thriving monastery had become dry and lifeless as brothers died and others served with heavy hearts. He asked the hermit: "Is it because of a sin that the monastery has been so diminished?" "Yes," came the answer, "the sin of ignorance. One of your members is the Messiah in disguise, and you are ignorant of this." Who could it be? How could this be? The Messiah in his midst and he did not recognize the Christ? Marveling the whole way home, the abbot thought of each member of the order. All had flaws. Yet one was the Messiah. On his return he assembled all the monks, telling them with amazement of the Messiah in their midst. Such an incredible honor! The Messiah in their midst, in disguise. They began to serve each other with great respect and consideration, knowing that one was the Christ. Soon their monastery glowed with grace and peace, goodness and joy. And countless were the seekers who came to their doors for guidance and admission.

The Cosmic Christ is here! Will you honor all whom you meet as the Messiah in disguise?

SUGGESTIONS FOR WORSHIP

Call to Worship

ONE: As nature sings God's praise, as the music of the spheres of heaven rings out,

MANY: So too may we praise our God who reigns today!

ONE: As birds in song rejoice, as rushing water dances,

MANY: So too may we praise our God who reigns today!

ONE: As all creation celebrates, as all who worship stand in awe,

MANY: So too may we praise our God who reigns today!

Prayer of Confession

Invisible God, made real in Jesus, we come to you for strength. You ask us to endure difficulty with patience; we grumble about hangnails. You ask us to give thanks with joyful hearts; we measure our blessings. You offer us sanctuary with the saints; we hide in the shadows. You reveal Christ to us throughout the world; we close our eyes, shut our ears, cut off our senses for we know that to absorb so great a reality would so completely change us. Give us strength to open our lives to you, to yield our hearts into your keeping. Amen.

Assurance of Pardon

God has rescued us from the power of darkness. In Christ we have redemption, the forgiveness of sins.

Benediction

May we go marveling with the strength of heaven, light of sun, radiance of moon, splendor of fire, speed of lightning, swiftness of wind, depth of sea, stability of earth, firmness of rock. May we go marveling in search of the Cosmic Christ hidden in plain sight.

1. Matthew Fox, *The Coming of the Cosmic Christ* (San Francisco: HarperSanFrancisco, 1988), 7.

Contributors

Nancy Ellett Allison is a Baptist minister who has served in a variety of ministerial roles as chaplain, missionary, professor, and pastor. She received her Ph.D. in pastoral theology from Southwestern Baptist Theological Seminary. Having recently moved with her family to Charlotte, North Carolina, she is serving as an intentional interim pastor, conflict mediator, and retreat leader with Baptist, Presbyterian, and United Church of Christ congregations. Her husband, Dale, is a church administrator. Together they parent teenage daughters, Carole and Laura.

Judith FaGalde Bennett is executive director of the Center for Congregational Ministry in Richmond, Virginia. A United Methodist pastor, she served churches in and around New York City for fifteen years and then served as associate general minister of the Virginia Council of Churches for eleven years. In addition to her present work, she also serves on the adjunct faculty of the School of Theology at Virginia Union University and as a writer of adult curriculum resources for The United Methodist Publishing House. Judy's previous careers included journalism, teaching, and dance. She is the mother of four and the grandmother of seven.

Jan Fuller Carruthers is University Chaplain and Assistant Professor of Religious Studies at Hollins University in Roanoke, Virginia, where she has served for the past fifteen years. Before going to Hollins, she was the Baptist Chaplain to Yale University for five years. Jan is the eldest daughter of Southern Baptist missionaries and was raised in Beirut, Lebanon. She has degrees from Hollins College, Yale University Divinity School, and Wesley Theological Seminary. She is affiliated with the Episcopal Church.

Wanda Burton-Crutchfield is the Executive Director of Area Christians Together in Service (ACTS) of Vance County (North Carolina), Inc. ACTS is a nonprofit, social ministry agency with a soup kitchen, pantry, homeless shelter, and comprehensive domestic violence service including safe shelter. Before coming to ACTS in 2001, Wanda served as pastor of Menokin Baptist in Warsaw, Virginia, for five years. She lives in Henderson, North Carolina, with her husband, John, who is also a minister whose specialty is Christian Education. Wanda is a graduate of Furman University and the Baptist Theological Seminary at Richmond and is a native of Iva, South Carolina.

Sue A. Ebersberger is designated pastor of Norriton Presbyterian Church in East Norriton, Pennsylvania. Sue was ordained several years ago at Bryn Mawr Presbyterian Church where she served as the associate pastor for singles, children, and their families. She "really learned to preach" as an interim pastor. Sue feels called to help people hear and fulfill Christ's calling in their lives by encouraging them to identify where their stories intersect the sacred stories of Scripture. Preaching is one way to do this! Prior to her ordained ministry, Sue was a corporate training manager for twelve years. She is the mother of a daughter, Grace, whom she adopted from China.

Kerra Becker English is the pastor of Juniata and Third Presbyterian Churches in Altoona, Pennsylvania. Kerra's ecclesial interests have included working on strategies for transformational ministries that will help churches find the voice that will truly speak to people in their darkest shadows and help them celebrate in their greatest joys. As a devoted student of theology, she contributed her pastoral insights to the "Institute for Reformed Theology" held at Union Theological Seminary and the Presbyterian School for Christian Education in Richmond, Virginia. She and her husband, Chuck, enjoy the delightful presence of their funny young son, Cade, who will one day be glad not to be a sermon illustration in this book.

Dusty Kenyon Fiedler is copastor of Covenant Presbyterian Church in Roanoke, Virginia. Dusty has enjoyed ministry for twenty-two years in tandem with her husband, Bob. (He even gave valuable advice on this project!) They also share in parenting two children and keeping the grass cut. Having traveled to fascinating place like Bangkok, Tunis, Edinburgh, and Jerusalem, Dusty also "lifts up my eyes to the hills" of her beloved Blue Ridge Mountains for a sense of the "wideness of God's mercy."

Kitty Cooper Holtzclaw is Minister of Worship and Evangelism at Buncombe Street United Methodist Church in Greenville, South Carolina. She is a full elder in the South Carolina Conference of the United Methodist Church and defines herself as the daughter of

157

Harold and Deane, the wife of George, the mother of Zachary, and as a friend, preacher, singer, reader, runner, and movie-goer.

Ruthanna B. Hooke is an Episcopal priest serving St. Paul's Church in Wallingford, Connecticut. She is also a doctoral student in theology at Yale University, currently completing her dissertation. Her dissertation investigates the relationship between divine and human activity in the event of preaching, reflecting on preaching through the theological themes of revelation, theological anthropology, and Christology. The inspiration for her theological studies, and for much of her preaching, comes from her background in the study of the Linklater voice method for actors, a method that helps actors restore their connection with the powerful and free voice with which they were born. Ruthanna hopes to use this method in her own future teaching of preachers.

Sandra Sonhyang Kim is pastor of Richmond Korean Presbyterian Church's English speaking ministry. She is also completing a Ph.D. in education at Union Theological Seminary and the Presbyterian School of Christian Education. She enjoys children of all ages (including her own preschool daughter, Eleanor, who provides many sermon illustrations!) and especially enjoys writing children's sermons.

Amy Louise Na is a Presbyterian minister and part-time chaplain for the Shenango Presbyterian Senior Care Home in New Wilmington, Pennsylvania. In 1991, the Presbytery of Philadelphia ordained her to be a mission specialist in Naples, Italy, where Amy was chaplain for a children's home, Casa Materna, and pastor for a small Methodist church. Following her time in Italy, she served as associate pastor of the Trinity Presbyterian Church in Cherry Hill, New Jersey. In addition to her part-time ministry, Amy serves as full-time mother to Christian, Laura, and Sofia. She and her family live in Neshannock Township, Pennsylvania, where Amy's husband, Kang, is a professor of religion at Westminster College.

Helen Nablo is an interim pastor in the Philadelphia area, currently serving the Overbrook Presbyterian Church. A graduate of Harvard and Vanderbilt Divinity Schools, she recently completed her Doctor of Ministry degree in preaching through McCormick Theological Seminary. She lives in Wayne, Pennsylvania, with her husband Mike Dunfee, also a Presbyterian pastor, and is mother to two and stepmother to three.

Teresa Lockhart Stricklen is Assistant Professor of Homiletics at Pittsburgh Theological Seminary where she also teaches worship. An ordained minister of the Presbyterian Church (U.S.A.), she has served several churches, including a small inner-city church, a fast-growing suburban church, a rural congregation, and a small church near Vanderbilt University where she received her Ph.D. in preaching and theology. She and her husband, two daughters, and border collie live in a big old Victorian house they are slowly restoring. Her interests are in the relationship of preaching and theology and its concomitant relationship to theological education and the church.

Dawn Darwin Weaks is senior pastor of First Christian Church in Rowlett, Texas. She is an ordained minister of the Christian Church (Disciples of Christ). Her husband, Joe, is also a Disciples minister. They were expecting their first child as these articles were written.

Marsha M. Wilfong is Assistant Professor of Homiletics and Worship at the University of Dubuque Theological Seminary. She is an ordained minister of the Presbyterian Church (U.S.A.) and has previously served for ten years as pastor of Presbyterian churches in Texas and Louisiana.

Index

Subject Index

Index

Scripture Index